What Has God Ever Done For Me?

What Has God Ever Done For Me?

God has done exactly what you and I could never do!

It is time to get face to face with a book,
which contains the truth of who you really are and
what God has done for you.

Colleen McLean

CONTENTS

INTRODUCTION

I have two pairs of glasses one pair is for everyday and they are multifocal which have three points of focus—for distance, intermediate and near vision. I also have glasses which have two points of focus, near and arm's length, which I wear when I am working at my desktop. Now occasionally if walk away from the computer with the wrong glasses on, my whole world is hopelessly distorted! The only thing I can see clearly is my hand in front of my face. We can look at the bible this way and only see a particular verse while the rest of the book is totally out of focus. I am guilty of taking verses out of their context and quoting them to explain a truth, however I hope that my surrounding discourse is sufficient to clarify the whole meaning. I state at the outset that anyone can unknowingly accept teaching, which later proves incorrect, and anyone can teach error without realizing it, or meaning harm.

I am reminded of Apollos in the book of Acts where we find Priscilla and Aquila "took (Apollos) aside and explained to him the way of God more accurately" (Acts 18:26). Apparently, the teaching Apollos received initially was inadequate, however he was willing to listen to a wife and husband team who teach him more accurately and as a result both he and the church greatly profited. God has given us His Word, the bible as a standard for discerning or dividing truth from error, this is why I encourage you to study His Word for yourself. The Bereans readily received the Word preached by Paul and Silas but they also "searched the scriptures daily to find out whether these things were so. Therefore many of them believed and also not a few of the Greeks, prominent women as well as men" (Acts 17:10–12). But, when the Jews from Thessalonica learned what was going on—they stirred up the crowds against Paul (see verse 13), and condemned his teaching without even checking to see if what Paul preached was true. The Bereans searched the scripture daily but the Jews from Thessalonica made no enquiry into the Scripture at all. They knew the content of the preaching at Berea and it enraged them to the point of stirring up violent opposition. Why? The bible tells us that they were envious and accused the Christians of turning their world upside down (see Acts 17:5, 6). The truth will turn our world right side up, and some may be incensed that their hypocrisy is exposed. If we could only realize the truth and the magnitude of what God has done not only for us but also for every individual believer on the planet for all time, it would transform us totally, and we would see things differently. Our world would be turned right side up!

This book is the result of wondering why so many beautiful Christians are generally ignorant of what has done for them personally and end up living a powerless Christianity. It is the result of wondering why leaders over the centuries could have believed that by applying scripture in a way that oppresses and disempowers people they were actually honoring God. This book is also the result of years of personal bible study, quietly plugging away every day and for the most part being unaware of where it would lead me. However, through it all, I always knew that I was God's workmanship, He planned my destiny and He filled me with the Holy Spirit so that I could have the pleasure of fulfilling his unique plan (see Eph 2:10). This I know that God also has a unique plan for you, no matter who you are or what you have done.

You have the pleasure of living it out and you are never too young or too old. My aim is to cause you to come alive to His unique plan for your life, to stir up God's love in you, to motivate you to come face to face with a book—the bible and thereby, discover the gift of undeserved, unearned grace. My aim is also to answer the question "what's God ever done for me?" and to reveal how and why these truths have been hidden, so that you will never be left wondering.

This book contains a scriptural list of the mighty things God has done for us. It is by no means exhaustive but it is truth. When I created this list, it took me about a year and at the end, I had changed, little by little. I discovered that depression no longer was a part of my life, I had more energy and I did not even realize it was happening.

By the time, you get to the end of this book you will know for sure what God has done for you. You will know the answers to the following—do I really matter to God? Does God really care about what is happening to me? In addition if I am called to run the race God has "marked out for me" (see Heb 12:1–2), how do I know which race to run? I pray you find yourself complete in Him, embrace His abundant grace and be confident in anything life can throw at you.

Much love
Colleen

Chapter 1

MICHAEL

Nineteen year-old Michael stood a short distance away from a street outreach team who were performing Christian songs and ministering to whoever cared to respond. People walked past him and he ignored them all. Looking intensely at the ground with anger on his face and tears in his eyes that were fogging up his broken glasses, Michael blurted out to the team, "What's God ever done for me?" His outbursts quickly turned into loud sobs, "I gave my life to Jesus, I believed in Him and look at me now, and I am homeless..." He could not continue as anger and painful memories were building up inside him, and spilling out in frustration, disappointment and to a certain degree hate. Time passed and then taking a step closer he cried out, "You Christians you...!" It seemed as if the memory was too painful to recall and his words faded. Just then I approached and began offering comfort, Michael rejected my offer, I backed off a little but persisted and asked if he knew Jesus. Michael replied, "Yeah, I know him, but what has He ever done for me?" Michael stared into space; his mind filled with the hard knocks he had taken shook his head and slumped to the ground. I sat down on the ground beside him and waited. I noticed the injury to his wrists. "What is that?" I asked, "The police arrested me and I resisted so they cuffed me." I asked, "Oh, have you been in trouble with the police?" Michael answered, "I can't remember what happened but I was in a rage, I was angry over something and they were called in to stop me. I suppose you are a Christian too?" I replied, "Yes, I am." Michael went on to say "And now you are going to tell me that God loves me, well just don't, because I have heard it all before, it is a joke!" I asked him what his name was, he answered readily enough. Then I asked, "Where do you live Michael?" He replied, "I used to live with a friend in a small flat, but he threw me out, now I sleep here and there." We sat together on the ground, just listening to the team singing, and finally I asked, "Can I pray for you?" Michael replied, "Whatever!" So I prayed for him, gave him my phone number, (which I never do) and said good bye."

Sometime later Michael contacted me and we chatted; gradually Michael softened. With every meeting, I prayed for him, washed his clothes, there was food to eat, and a shower to freshen up. I lost touch with Michael, but the question—"What has Jesus ever done for me" troubled me. I knew that the magnitude of what Jesus accomplished at the cross is foolishness to the natural mind, but Michael was born again, how did he not understand what God had done for him?

Unfortunately, I soon discovered that well-meaning religious people have distorted the truth of the Gospel message, and in some cases, made it so difficult to understand that it is out of the reach of the average person. Only the really super holy people get to have the experience. This was Michael's dilemma; he did not allow himself to feel the wonderful life changing experience of an encounter with God because he thought he could never be good enough to deserve it. Michael thought that God was so mighty and exalted in power and majesty, that God would not be friends with him. The truth is God's burning desire was for Michael to hear His voice and relate to him personally. The truth is that Jesus was friends with people who were just like Michael—Jesus loved them and loved to be around them, He healed them and they followed him. The truth is that Michael did not know how much he was loved, accepted, forgiven, qualified and equal to the holiest person alive or dead. Michael did not know that it was not because of anything he did but because of what Jesus did over 2000 years ago.

When we do not know what God has done for us, we rely on our own resources and ask God to bless it, and we end up praying for things we already have, or we attempt to achieve our salvation by doing good works and then the slippery slope begins. The truth is that God's love through what Jesus has done demonstrates how valuable we are, not our works. There is nothing left for us to do except believe! Therefore to answer the question what has God ever done for me means nothing if you do not have a clue or you do not care to understand what it all means. Ignorance can also be an excuse to live in denial of Christianity. We live in denial because we are afraid to face our vulnerability, our lack and our built in need to worship something bigger.

Michael was in denial because he could not face what he believed to be too painful and that God would not listen anyway. He could not face the fact that he was living in the consequences of his actions and that God had nothing to do with it. Yet, God is always there to lead us out, but He was not the One who gave Michael the pain and heartache. By the way, God will never force His help upon us.

Michael's problem lies in a wrong impression of what it means to be loved by God, so in fact he genuinely did not know what God had done for him and sadly no one took the time to lovingly disciple him in the ways of the Father's love. Some men never know what it means to have a father who loved them when they were growing up. Many never experienced approval from their dads, so they find it hard to accept God's acceptance, love and approval. For many men and indeed women the father word stirs up all the wrong emotions. Men especially suffer from 'the absent father' syndrome where a lack of fathering leaves a hole in their hearts, that leaves them looking for approval and acceptance in all the wrong places. Many men grow up to hate their fathers because of the way they failed them. The answer is simply in finding God's abundant grace to forgive. If God is so quick to forgive our mistakes and restore what we have lost, then it cannot be that hard to forgive our absent dads, after all God wants us to relate to Him as a father.

John the Apostle referred to himself as "the apostle Jesus loved." It was impossible for Jesus to love John more than the others, however, John saw himself this way. He wrote in his first letter chapter 3 verse 1 "Behold what manner of love the Father has bestowed on us, that we should be called children of God!" Michael could not see himself as one Jesus loves or as a child of God. He had the impression that God was angry with him for his rebellion and lack of upright living. Michael did not really know the Father's love and that God does not hold grudges—He is totally accepting, no matter what we have done. The Father promised that no matter what—once invited into anyone's life, by faith, believing that Jesus sacrifice is sufficient for salvation—He would never leave.

So how does Michael get out of this predicament? Finding a safe place to chat without judgment and being 'preached at' is a good start. Christians should be good at this but in Michael's case it seems they let him down. Without this safe place to be honest,

Michael buried his pain, blamed God for it and walked away. It was fear of punishment and the judgement of Christians, which sent Michael down this path and away from the church but not away from God's unending love and forgiveness.

The Book of Numbers chapter 21 tells us that during the wilderness journey, the Israelites became discouraged and they murmured and complained against God and Moses, much the same way as Michael did. Numbers 21:5 "And the people spoke against God and against Moses: "Why have you brought us up out of Egypt to die in the wilderness? For there is no food and no water, and our soul loathes this worthless bread." I can hear the Israelite people saying, "What has God ever done for me, look at me I am homeless out here in this stupid desert with worthless bread to eat, and God gave me Moses to help me and, so on." This is a good question and it deserves a good answer. What had God done for them?

The bible tells us—He delivered them from a life of slavery in Egypt, protected them from Pharaoh's army with a pillar of fire and parted the Red Sea for them to pass through. Yet the people still complained and even called the manna God provided worthless bread, which they loathed. Yet they ate it for forty years and their feet did not swell, not did their clothes wear out and not one of them got sick (see Deut 8:4, 29:5). You could say they were ungrateful! God has done the same thing for us today all because of the suffering, death, resurrection, ascension of Jesus, and the sending of the Holy Spirit. We have been delivered from a life of slavery to sin when we were born again (see Rom 6:6, 22), Jesus defeated the enemy's army at the cross and resurrected us from our old life at our water baptism (see Romans 6:12; Colossians 2:12). He has placed us in the Kingdom of the Son of His love (see Col 1:13), gave us His Holy Spirit to empower us to not only take our Promised Land, but to comfort, teach and remind us of everything Jesus said (see John 14:26, 15:26, 16:7). He Himself gave us apostles, prophets, evangelists, pastors and teachers to equip us for the work of ministry (see Eph 4:11–12). Could you say that we are sometimes ungrateful? I would say, yes because like the Israelites we forget and do not give God significance in our lives.

Search the scriptures for yourself—get face to face with a book that contains the truth of who you really are in God and what He has done for you. The Israelites spent time everyday collecting manna for food. This was God's idea, not a religious ritual or a rule devised by a leader or denomination for their people to perform. God's idea is for us to understand fully what the finished work of Jesus means to us personally, and this will take our time, especially if we have learnt wrongly that God is angry with us and is ever ready to punish us. He is the true bread/manna from heaven and only He satisfies (John 6:32–33). Jesus is the author and finisher of our faith, so we look to Him (see Heb 12:2).

Numbers chapter 21 continues with the story—Numbers 21:6 "So the LORD sent fiery serpents among the people, and they bit the people; and many of the people of Israel died." Remember this was the Old covenant, not the New Covenant in Jesus Blood, which you and I walk in today. Then Numbers 21:7–8 "Therefore the people came to Moses, and said, "We have sinned, for we have spoken against the LORD and against you; pray to the LORD that He take away the serpents from us." So Moses prayed for the people. Then the LORD said to Moses, "Make a fiery serpent, and set it on a pole; and it shall be that everyone who is bitten, when he looks at it, shall live."

The serpent on the pole is a picture of Jesus on the cross. Jesus drew the comparison Himself when He said, "When Moses lifted up the serpent in the wilderness, even so the Son of Man must be lifted up and whoever believes in Him should not perish but have eternal life" (John 3:14-15). God suspended Jesus between heaven and earth for the whole world to look at and live. Whoever looks on Jesus and sees their sins and sicknesses on Him has forgiveness forever. This truth sets us free from the futility and hopelessness of wandering in the world. The truth is that God's love for you is real and in His eyes you are blameless (see 1 Cor 15:34) no matter what you have done or not done.

At one point I even resigned myself to spending eternity in hell because I thought there was no way God would ever forgive me. There was another time when I believed that when I sinned God could not even look at me until I confessed and received forgiveness. I was taught that my sin was the only thing that could separate me from God, even though the bible says that nothing in the whole universe has power to separate me from God's love, or stop God loving me or diminishing his love for me (Romans 8:35, 38-39). I now believe that 'nothing' includes my sin, rebellion, mistakes, my bad choices, pride and ignorance.

You can be sure of this—there is absolutely no thing that can come between you and God's love. "Who shall separate me from the love of Christ? Shall tribulation, or distress, or persecution, or famine, or nakedness, or peril, or sword…? For I am persuaded that neither death nor life, nor angels nor principalities nor powers, nor things present nor things to come, nor height nor depth, nor any other created thing, shall be able to separate us from the love of God which is in Christ Jesus our Lord" (Romans 8:35, 38–39). Nothing and no one can separate you from God's love. It does not matter if you are in the worst circumstance or the best situation that life can throw at you.

Believing God loves you no matter what has to make a difference in your life. Knowing and believing what God has done for you, knowing the Author of your salvation, believing that you are a son or daughter of the King of kings has to cause you to stand tall and conquer anything that comes your way. Paul the Apostle wrote that God has made you to be not just a conqueror but also more than a conqueror (see Romans 8:37). It is all simply by grace through faith for your whole life, because nothing and no one can snatch you out of His hand.

Chapter 2

ARTHUR

Here is a depiction of a middle-aged man, named Arthur, who was thought well of in the community, he was a well-known Christian, serving as a deacon in the local church. Life was good until he encountered dysfunction in his family. He took the problem upon himself, tried to fix it and did not consult his wife. He had the answers to the problem, and he thought he was right and if everyone did things his ways, life would be good again. Unfortunately, he only made matters worse. At the same time, his church ministry became more demanding and someone suggested that he needed the baptism in the Holy Spirit; he resisted their advice because he thought he already had it and what would they know anyway. Arthur struggled in his own strength and still is today and things have not changed. What Arthur needed to realize was that in his own strength there is no grace to help, no righteousness, peace or joy. The apostle Paul considered all his accomplishments, his own strengths and righteous deeds as dung (see Phil 3:8), while the Old Testament prophet Isaiah considered "all our righteousness are like filthy rags (see Isa 64:6).

Arthur's problem lies in a wrong impression of what it means to be a husband and father. His culture taught him to be the leader, have all the right answers, build ministries and rule his family with an iron fist. He fully believed that the Bible qualified him be the boss of his marriage, family and ministry, which put unbelievable pressure upon him. The church he belonged to cited Ephesians 5:23 as well as 1 Corinthians 11:3 as the standard by which he was to conduct his affairs.

Surely, marriage has to be about serving each other. God's design for marriage is about being one, where one is not under or over the other one. Marriage is a partnership of equals where both husband and wife rule together over creation, not each other (see Gen 1:27–28). The original plan, has not changed, it has always been divine unity, equality and mutual, and voluntary submission. Jesus taught his followers that they were to be different to the prevailing culture of male domination. His words recorded for us to read in the gospels of Matthew, Mark and Luke.

> "But Jesus called them to Himself and said, "You know that the rulers of the Gentiles lord it over them, and those who are great exercise authority over them. Yet it shall not be so among you; but whoever desires to become great among you, let him be your servant and whoever desires to be first among you, let him be your slave—just as the Son of Man did not come to be served, but to serve, and to give His life a ransom for many" (Matt 20:25–28).

What Arthur did not realize is that the Holy Spirit, flowing out of him helps him to speak God's wisdom into the situation. Arthur's achievements and popularity were the result his own hard work but at the same time, he craved acceptance and validation. For Arthur it was all about deserving, doing, working and being busy trying to win the approval of God and the community. For Michael it was all about complaining, murmuring and largely ignorance.

Michael and Arthur did not know what God had already done for them—they did not understand that God gives grace and righteousness to them freely (Rom 5:17), undeservedly, unconditionally and fully, there are no half measures, and it does not matter who you are, male or female, child or teenager, or what you have done or not done. Michael and Arthur did not know the Father's heart towards them much like the two brothers in the parable of the Prodigal Son.

Chapter 3

THE FATHER'S HEART

We find a true picture of The Father's heart in the parables of the lost sheep, the lost son, and the lost coin in the Gospel of Luke chapter 15. Notice here that the one that was lost never lost value, the son, the sheep and the coin were at all times extremely valuable and so very worthy to be found, and restored.

A basic principle of bible study and interpretation is to ask the question "Does this make sense to the people to whom it was written?" The text must make sense to its original hearers. So with this in mind let's look at the parables told by Jesus to the tax collectors, sinners and Pharisees and scribes, who drew near to hear what He was saying (see Luke 15:1–2). To them it was a real life illustration, which revealed a truth about them and the Father's love.

The Lost Sheep

In this parable, the shepherd is Jesus, the lost sheep are the notorious sinners who are listening to Jesus and whom the religious leaders are complaining about, the ninety-nine sheep left in the sheep pen are the so-called righteous Pharisees.

"What man of you, having a hundred sheep, if he loses one of them, does not leave the ninety-nine in the wilderness, and go after the one which is lost until he finds it? And when he has found it, he lays it on his shoulders, rejoicing and when he comes home, he calls together his friends and neighbors, saying to them, 'Rejoice with me, for I have found my sheep which was lost!' I say to you that likewise there will be more joy in heaven over one sinner who repents than over ninety-nine just persons who need no repentance" (Luke 15:4).

One sheep was so completely lost it had no hope of finding anything, even food and certainly not protection. The shepherd searched for it until he found it, and when he did find it he did not scold or punish it, he laid it upon his shoulders, carried it home and rejoiced with his friends. To the corrupt tax collectors and the other known sinners who gathered around to listen, it was a good news story because the rabbis, scribes and Pharisees excluded them from the religious community and if they ever heard anything, it was always condemnation. However, it was a bad news story for the religious leaders because they were the experts and they shunned sinners.

We have to be aware here that the religious leaders taught and enforced the law and there was no love, compassion or forgiveness in their teaching. Furthermore, in their zeal for the law their attitude was merely external. Everything Jesus did and said exposed their blatant hypocrisy; their pride and sense of male superiority (see Matt 6:2, 5, 16; Mat 15:7 and chapter 23).

The Lost Coin

The woman in the parable represents the Holy Spirit. The lost coin represents the sinners who Jesus was speaking to and who He intentionally went out on the streets to find. The nine coins represent the Pharisees and scribes who see themselves as righteous.

Luke 15:8-10

> "Or what woman, having ten silver coins, if she loses one coin, does not light a lamp, sweep the house, and search carefully until she finds it? And when she has found it, she calls her friends and neighbors together, saying, 'Rejoice with me, for I have found the piece which I lost!' Likewise, I say to you, there is joy in the presence of the angels of God over one sinner who repents."

Jesus further upset his religious listeners with this shocking parable. Shocking because Jesus used the woman as a metaphor for God. The woman searched for the lost coin diligently and carefully until she found it, she made sure no one else would find it and claim it. Jesus came from the Father to seek and save the lost (see Luke 19:10; Matt 18:11), He did not come to judge but to save. He sent the Holy Spirit to call out the lost ones, to guide and comfort. When the lost one is found, there is only great joy, there is not even a hint of condemnation nor disapproval just joy! There is no fear here!

The Prodigal Son

The prodigal represents the sinners who are friends of Jesus and who are following Him around. The Father represents God. The elder son represents the religious leaders who want everyone punished for their sins.

Luke 15:11-32

> Then He said: "A certain man had two sons. And the younger of them said to his father, 'Father, give me the portion of goods that falls to me.' So he divided to them his livelihood. And not many days after, the younger son gathered all together, journeyed to a far country, and there wasted his possessions with prodigal living. But when he had spent all, there arose a severe famine in that land, and he began to be in want. Then he went and joined himself to a citizen of that country, and he sent him into his fields to feed swine. And he would gladly have filled his stomach with the pods that the swine ate, and no one gave him anything. "But when he came to himself, he said, 'How many of my father's hired servants have bread enough and to spare, and I perish with hunger! I will arise and go to my father, and will say to him, "Father, I have sinned against heaven and before you, and I am no longer worthy to be called your son. Make me like one of your hired servants." "And he arose and came to his father. But when he was still a great way off, his father saw him and had compassion, and ran and fell on his neck and kissed him. And the son said to him, 'Father, I have sinned against heaven and in your sight, and am no longer worthy to be

called your son.' "But the father said to his servants, 'Bring out the best robe and put it on him, and put a ring on his hand and sandals on his feet. And bring the fatted calf here and kill it, and let us eat and be merry; for this my son was dead and is alive again; he was lost and is found.' And they began to be merry. "Now his older son was in the field. And as he came and drew near to the house, he heard music and dancing. So he called one of the servants and asked what these things meant. And he said to him, 'Your brother has come, and because he has received him safe and sound, your father has killed the fatted calf.' "But he was angry and would not go in. Therefore his father came out and pleaded with him. So he answered and said to his father, 'Lo, these many years I have been serving you; I never transgressed your commandment at any time; and yet you never gave me a young goat that I might make merry with my friends. But as soon as this son of yours came, who has devoured your livelihood with harlots, you killed the fatted calf for him.' "And he said to him, 'Son, you are always with me, and all that I have is yours. It was right that we should make merry and be glad, for your brother was dead and is alive again, and was lost and is found.'"

The lost son parable is all about the father's heart towards his two sons. In those days, it was a great offense for a son to ask his father for his inheritance. It would be equivalent to saying, "I wish you were already dead!"[1] Both sons received their inheritance (Luke 15:12) with the eldest son receiving two-thirds (see Deut 21:17). The story goes on to show us the younger son left home and lived the prodigal lifestyle while the older son continued working on the farm.

The prodigal son after squandering his inheritance returns home because he was hungry and he thought that if his father would hire him as a servant, then he would escape punishment and have plenty of good food to eat. However, that was all completely undone when the father heaped upon him unconditional love with an embrace, the abundance of grace and the gift of righteousness and received him home with celebration.

The older brother, returning at the end of a long day's work was angry and resentful that his brother received such undeserved favor, instead of punishment. Furthermore, he proceeds to humiliate and insult his father by refusing to go to the welcome home party. Keep in mind here that the older brother had nothing to lose by entering the house, as he had already received his inheritance.

Both sons did not know their father's heart towards them, the younger son wanted to work for his food and keep his pride by coming home as a hired servant, he never expressed any gratitude or love for his father. For the older brother it was all about how dutifully he had served his father all these years and how the father never gave him a party, but he never expressed any gratitude or love for his father either.

Both brothers mistakenly believed that they had to earn their father's love and approval, by serving. The prodigal even admitted that he was not worthy to be his father's son. Everyone is someone's son or daughter and you don't have to be worthy or work for it, you just are. The 'best robe' that the father put on his son was his own robe and it is a picture of righteousness. The son did not earn it, work for it nor deserve it. It was a gift! The 'ring' was the seal of sonship, freely given. 'Sandals' were not worn by slaves, so there was no way the father would allow his son to be a hired servant.

The 'fatted calf' would have fed the whole village, it was going to be a big party but it would be a happy/sad celebration for the father because his beloved eldest son threw a silent tantrum and refused to attend.

The father in the parable is Father God and the lesson for us is life changing. When we encounter such acceptance, love, mercy, forgiveness and grace when we are very undeserving of it, it has to affect the way we continue to conduct our lives. It is never all about us or our love for God it is always about Jesus, his finished work on the cross and God's never-ending, unlimited and lavish love for us.

Look at the testimony of Paul.

> "Although I was formerly a blasphemer, a persecutor, and an insolent man; but I obtained mercy because I did it ignorantly in unbelief. And the grace of our Lord was exceedingly abundant, with faith and love which are in Christ Jesus. This is a faithful saying and worthy of all acceptance, that Christ Jesus came into the world to save sinners, of whom I am chief."
> (1 Tim 1:13–15).

By his own admission, he claimed that he was the chief of sinners, an insolent man who hated Christians enough to kill them. He had no problem imprisoning them; including women (see Acts 8:3). He had the reputation of a terrorist, yet it made no difference to God; the grace and love of our Lord was exceedingly abundant toward him. Not only did Paul escape the punishment he deserved, he received abundant kindness, acceptance and forgiveness. God will do the same for you. Where sin abounds, grace abounds even more (see Rom 5:20). You can be sure that Jesus Christ came into the world to save even the worst of sinners—this surely is amazing grace! The truth is that while we were far from God, in the pig pen of pride and selfishness, God demonstrated His own love toward us by sending Jesus to die for us, in our place (Rom 5:8). Why would our Father God do this? Because of His great love! (See Eph 2:4).

The Father's heart is just, merciful and extremely fair, it is so merciful and fair that He does not hold sin against us, He does not deal with us according to our sins nor can He punish us, because He has removed our sins from us as far as the east is from the west (Psalm 103:12). That means that we don't get what we deserve because Jesus got what we deserve. Jesus paid the debt 'once and for all!' Only a loving, and compassionate, God could have done this, no other so called god in the whole of time and the universe has the power, authority or will to do this ever. There is none like Him! "Among the gods there is none like You, O Lord; nor are there any works like Your works" (see Psalm 86:8). David, the writer of this psalm knew that Yahweh stood in absolute contrast to every other pagan god; there was none like Yahweh! Nor were there any works that comparable to Yahweh's works, because His works demonstrate His great love.

Chapter 4

WHERE DID IT ALL GO WRONG?

Where did it all go wrong? In their book "The World's Greatest Revivals" authors Fred and Sharon Wright [2]write about the two components that every major revival features. First, revival emphasizes essential truths about the nature and purposes of God that have been ignored, discarded, or lost by successive generations of professing believers and well-meaning church leaders and theologians. Second, the revival is spurred on by hungry and desperate people who are seeking answers to their needs, the Church's needs, and society's needs."

The Reformation in the 1500s highlighted a forgotten truth about Jesus Christ as the only means of Salvation. The First Great Awakening in the 1700s restored the truth that the Church needs to fulfil the Great Commission. The Pentecostal Revival of Azusa Street in 1906 restored the truth of the empowering of the Holy Spirit. The Father Heart Revival released in Toronto restored the truth that we need to experience the Love of God the Father and enjoy intimacy with Him.[3]

A heresy that sparked the Protestant Reformation was that women needed a mediator other than Christ. Many people were cruelly tortured and martyred defending the truth that believers in Christ do not need human go-betweens. However, in the mid-1600s in England, a revival movement began that released women to minister in unprecedented ways. George Fox of the Quakers, believed that since the Holy Spirit dwells in men and women alike, and since it is He who rightly interprets the Bible, both genders have the same capacity to speak for God.[4]

In the next three hundred years, God reiterated through other nascent revival movements that He could use women. Methodism, the Holiness Movement, the Salvation Army, and the Pentecostal Outpouring each opened the door to women to step beyond the roles of family to impact the church and society.[5]

In the Middle Ages the bible was used to condemn witchcraft, unfortunately those accused were denied fair trials, they were tortured, burned at the stake or drowned. "One bishop in Germany claimed to have killed nineteen hundred witches in five years. A Lutheran leader, Benedict Carpzov, claimed to have sentenced twenty thousand devil worshipers to death—most of them female. One historical account suggests that the female population of two French villages—all except two women—was wiped out."[6]

In South Africa, leaders of the Dutch Reformed church used passages in Genesis to teach that black people are actually animals, not humans. In Hitler's Germany, some Christians used the bible to defend acts of violence against Jewish people—saying that Jews deserved punishment because they were responsible for Christ's crucifixion. Before the American Civil War, some sincere Christians used the words of the apostle Paul in Ephesians 6:2 and Colossians 3:22 and an Old Testament passage Exo 22:18 to support the practice of slavery and to outlaw interracial marriage. Some bible teachers have taught that God no longer performs healing or other miracles mentioned in the Book of

Acts. Many Christian denominations have taken obscure Bible verses such as 1 Timothy 2:9 out of context to create legalistic dress codes. The bible was used again, to deny women the right to own property, leaving them homeless if their husband died or they were divorced. In the 1800s church leaders opposed the higher education of women and in some nations the right to vote by quoting 1 Timothy 2:12 and actually used Ephesians 5:22 to justify wife beating.[7] This is abuse in the extreme!

What motivated church leaders to commit these atrocities and even worse use the bible to justify their actions? How did we get to a place of total domination of the masses who blindly believe women and people with black skin are inferior or that God condones wife beating, slavery and slaughter of innocent people? How is it then that the Word of God is so distorted and people like Michael have to ask the question—"What has God ever done for me?" Sometimes when well-intentioned leaders distort the Word of God in a misguided attempt to make people obey rules in order to be right with God and/or for personal gain. Legalism wants people to do the right thing. This implies that all God wants from us is to live a moral life and obey the commandments. This approach is not God focused, it is self-focused and pride driven. This pride has led to keeping people ignorant concerning their freedom in Christ, and thus the need for revival. However, the Word of God will not be stopped, and unfortunately, many of us do not appreciate or realize what a privilege it is, to have access to the Bible in an understandable form. Dr Brian Simmons writes—"The message of grace that the Apostle preached was not second-hand truth that he got from someone else, for he received it through a direct encounter with Jesus. Paul's ministry can be trusted and his gospel can be believed."[8]. "God longs for us to know Him and love Him. The Fact that He wants to be loved, worshiped and served must burn its way into our hearts through the written inspired Word of God."[9]

Chapter 5

THE CULPRIT

The culprit in a sentence is the pride in humankind that attaches itself to legalism. What do I mean by legalism? Legalism is simply the divisive doctrines of men, because it is all about what we do, as opposed to what Jesus has done. Legalism is like a wet blanket thrown over the fire in the hearts of God's people, and results is many wondering what God has really done for them. It stifles inspiration, revelation and leaves us with obligations, rules and punishment when we cannot fulfil its demands. These rules, bind heavy loads on people and they have no value in bringing us closer to God.

Our identity and significance is not in what we do. Our identity is in Jesus—in his suffering, death, resurrection, ascension and the sending of the Holy Spirit in power. Real Christianity is God reaching down to us because of His great love, not us reaching up to God by trying to be holy by keeping rules. Rule keeping cannot make us holy. 1 Corinthians 3:16-17 says that your body is a temple of the Holy Spirit, and that the Spirit of God dwells in you. Verse 17 says that "the temple of God is holy, which temple you are." We may not always feel holy, and it is just as well that the truth is not determined by what we feel, it is determined by what God says about us—we became holy by the finished work of Jesus. Heb 10:10 says that, "We have been sanctified through the offering of the body of Jesus Christ once for all." Paul called the badly behaved Corinthians, and the people of Achaia 'saints' (see 2 Cor 1:1). He addressed his letter to the Ephesians—"to the saints" (see Eph 1:1). Their holiness had nothing to do with what they did. Paul reminded the Corinthians that their righteousness and sanctification and redemption was all by God's doing (see 1 Cor 1:30).

If there is a line to be drawn, it has to be here—between grace and legalism, between the Old Covenant and New Covenant. The New Testament clearly has grace and truth in the person of Jesus Christ (see John 1:17) on the same side of the line. The New Covenant is where God writes His laws on our hearts and not on stone (see Jere 31:33). However, sadly in some churches you will find human philosophy and legalism added to Christianity. This is like adding new wine to old wineskins; the wine is spilled, and the wineskins are ruined (see Mark 2:22).

Jesus was speaking to the disciples of John and the disciples of the Pharisees when He said, "The days will come..." He was giving them a glimpse of the new covenant, which was coming. He continued, "No one sews a piece of unshrunk cloth on an old garment; or else the new piece pulls away from the old, and the tear is made worse and no one puts new wine into old wineskins; or else the new wine bursts the wineskins, the wine is spilled, and the wineskins are ruined. But new wine must be put into new wineskins." (Mark 2:20-22).

Jesus did not come to make the Old Covenant better He came to do away with it all together. He did not come to patch up an old garment, He came to introduce something completely new— new clothes and new wine for a new person. You cannot fit this new life in Christ into the Old Covenant and if you do, both are ruined. The Old Covenant is completely incompatible with the new, and God never intended to patch it up. The old wineskins represents the Old Covenant of Law and the rituals of Judaism, the new garment and the new wine represents our new life under grace. Law and grace are opposites it is either one or the other, the old or the new, either hot or cold. Rev 3:16 says, "So then, because you are lukewarm, and neither cold nor hot, I will vomit you out of My mouth." God would have us either hot or cold because lukewarm is a mixture of hot and cold, or the mixture of law and grace. Hot is walking in grace, cold is walking in the law. God would rather we be stone cold and walking in the Law which was written in cold stone because "the law was our tutor to bring us to Christ, that we might be justified by faith" (Gal 3:24). So of course, at least we have an opportunity to be justified by faith in Jesus if we are cold.

Illustration—In Australia every house has a back yard and a front yard which is covered with grass, and every home has a lawn mower and the lawns are mowed regularly to keep the grass from taking over the yard and so the children can play. So imagine for a moment that the lawn mower represents grace and the long grass represents sin. As long as you have a mower, there is no problem. Then you need to dig up the old stone drive way because it needs replacing and lumps of stone which represent the law are spread all over the front yard. It is now impossible to use the mower (grace) to cut the long grass (sin) which is still growing up and around the broken up pieces of stone (law). The moral of the story—grace (lawn mower) is useless when law (stone) is present. Law and grace therefore, is a mixture and God hates mixture.

The Galatian church in the first century was guilty of mixing grace and law and Paul called them foolish.

> O foolish Galatians! Who has bewitched you that you should not obey the truth, before whose eyes Jesus Christ was clearly portrayed among you as crucified? This only I want to learn from you: Did you receive the Spirit by the works of the law, or by the hearing of faith?—Are you so foolish? Having begun in the Spirit, are you now being made perfect by the flesh?" (Gal 3:1–3)

Today I would say, "Use your brains people!" How did you first receive the Spirit? Think about this—you received salvation as a free gift, you began in the freedom of the Spirit, as a new creation, fully, freely and forever forgiven, and now you want to forsake it all and go back and instead be made perfect by keeping the Commandments in your own strength?" NOT! To say salvation is by God's grace but you have to keep all the commandments or you will lose your salvation is foolishness. It is grace mixed with law. Then what hope have we got. How can we find the answer to what God has ever done for us, if we are without hope?

This is so serious Paul wrote in very strong language and repeated himself—

> "But even if we, or an angel from heaven, preach any other gospel to you than what we have preached to you, let him be accursed. As we have said before, so now I say again, if anyone preaches any other gospel to you than what you have received, let him be accursed" (Gal 1:8–9).

Clearly then the different gospel of mixing grace and law is a perversion and it opens the door for the enemy to further persuade vulnerable Christians to trust in their own efforts at cleaning themselves up and thereby keeping them ignorant of what God has done for them.

In Galatians chapter 2 Paul explained clearly what justifies us. Here it is—

> "Knowing that a man is not justified by the works of the law but by faith in Jesus Christ, even we have believed in Christ Jesus, that we might be justified by faith in Christ and not by the works of the law; for by the works of the law no flesh shall be justified" (Gal 2:16).

The Galatians turned away from the gospel of grace because some people were teaching a false gospel. The cross of Jesus Christ is so powerful that when believed it will separate us forever from guilt and every curse. God loves us into wholeness/holiness and it is all by grace through faith and it that is why it cannot ever be through our effort at law keeping and trying to clean ourselves up. Every person—saved and unsaved needs to hear the truth that all they need is a Savior and all they have to do is believe. It is faith and faith alone and it always will be! God will only ever offer salvation by grace through faith in Jesus Christ because it is a gift (see Eph 2:8).

Somehow, Michael believed the lie that to please God he had to change his life but he was powerless to do so. He tried and failed, and tried and failed and this led him to believe Christianity was a joke because he would never be good enough for God to love him. For Arthur it was the lie that he must be qualified by keeping the Ten Commandments and performing good works, instead of resting in what God has already done or him. They both believed they had to measure up to what society believes it is to be a man.

They wanted to live a holy life, but they did not know that in their own strength it is impossible to achieve. Most definitely, we are to live holy lives and that is why God provided us with abundant grace to face every temptation that comes our way and therefore experience the victory over it. "Grace is undeserved, unmerited, unearned favor of God—the moment you try to merit the free favors of God, His grace is nullified,[10]" so when striving in your own strength starts the flow of grace stops.

Chapter 6

TRUTH DESTROYED AND TRUTH RESTORED

Every misinterpretation or misrepresentation of scripture I can think of is a rejection of grace and truth, and that leads to legalism, which involves punishment. History shows that it is possible to lose sight of the whole truth of the Gospel, but history also shows that God re-establishes His truth about Himself and His purposes in the church. "The Reformation of the 1500's restored the truth that Jesus Christ is the only means of Salvation, "that justification is based on faith alone, that righteousness is found only in Christ Jesus Himself and is continually imputed to the account of believing man, that Holy Scriptures are the sole authority for faith and practice, and that the believer needs not to pray through a priest or saint but can confess sin and pray directly to God.[11]" We are still living in the truth of Martin Luther's 95 theses and still fulfilling the Great Commission and the Baptism in the Holy Spirit. We are experiencing the Father's love, and releasing women to fulfil their God given destiny.

If we are going to reach people who genuinely do not know what God has done for them, we must break with legalism and biases that limit the truth, and instead embrace the whole Gospel of

Grace. Why? Because there will always be people like Michael and Arthur who have a heart for God, who are desperately in search of Truth and Grace, and need some human help along the way. We must also be sensitive to their needs and culture. The bible does not give us a standard dress code or codes of behavior for worship so the danger is in making our standards so high that ordinary people feel alienated. The danger is in presenting to the people a set of rules rather than a personal relationship with God.

Just as the Baptism of the Holy Spirit, the operation of the gifts of the Spirit, the free gift of grace and righteousness, faith, and personal holiness have decayed and been revived over the years, some of the church has still given place to spiritual pride, prejudice, legalism and control. In so doing they have crushed seekers from a passionate relationship with the Lord Jesus and people like Michael and Arthur are left asking the question—what has God ever done for me?

On the other hand accepting God's grace and His favor leads to thankfulness and heart-felt worship. After all God promised to write *His* laws on our hearts and not on stone anymore (see Jer 31:33–34). Jesus went beyond the Law and revealed God's intention—the sacrifices and atonement pointed to Himself. Jesus was the fulfilment of everything in the Old Testament.

Chapter 7

DROP THE ROCKS

In the Gospel of John chapter 8, we read about the woman caught in adultery where Jesus extended His forgiveness and gave her the gift of no condemnation. The Pharisees dragged this woman and threw her at the feet of Jesus. Think about this for a moment, to be caught committing adultery, the Pharisees would have had to enter the bedroom, witness the act and drag her out. She was most likely naked. This was a deliberately planned and executed. Their intention was twofold first to test Jesus, that they might have something of which to accuse Him, and second to stone the woman to death citing the Law of Moses as their motivation for doing so (see Lev 20:10). Jesus said, "He who is without sin among you, let him be the first to throw a stone at her." One by one, they dropped their stones and left. Jesus said, "Woman, where are your accusers? Has no one condemned you?" She replied, "No one Lord." Jesus said "Neither do I condemn you; go and sin no more" (see John 8:7–11). The woman at His feet received what she did not deserve; she knew she had sinned, she was aware of her sin—God loved her anyway! Jesus freely forgave her and gave her the gift of no condemnation. She was not condemned, she was free to go and sin no more. (Notice Jesus never condoned her sin). Some of us need to drop the rocks, and realize that Jesus is the answer and stop using the bible to condemn and crush those who fail because we all sin, none of us is without sin, and we all need a Savior.

Jesus never told the precious people he healed and delivered from all kinds of sin and immorality that hell was waiting for them if they did not turn to Him, rather He demonstrated His goodness and love toward them. The goodness of God will lead people to change their minds about Him (see Rom 2:4). God initiates with His goodness and unconditional love, and we respond by changing our minds.

Enthusiastic and well-meaning preachers spread the word saying, drunks, homosexuals, adulterers, liars, fornicators, thieves, atheists, and idolaters that hell awaits them unless they repent and turn to Jesus. In my opinion, this does not win anyone because the command to repent comes with the connotation that you have to clean yourself up, beat yourself up, and show some super sorrow before you can even think about coming to Jesus to escape hell. Well that is never going to happen—there is no way anyone can save themselves from their sin first then turn to Jesus. Not even the Holy Spirit will remind people of their sin because sin is not the problem, Jesus took away the sins of the whole world and God will not remember them (see John 1:29, Heb 8:12). The problem is in rejecting what Jesus has done for them.

Christians have to drop the rocks because this attitude causes people to run from God not to Him. Instead of having an encounter with God they experience a set of rules, regulations and repentance—a word they do not understand at all, and that does not inspire hope. Instead of experiencing intimacy with the Lord that changes them on the inside, they experience separation and judgment, which drives them deeper into hopelessness. It was not the knowledge of sin that gave the woman caught in the act of adultery the freedom to go and sin no more, it was the gift of no condemnation and the love of Jesus that changed her forever.

By the way, repentance simply means to change your mind and it only works in an environment of grace. It is useless in a judgmental, rule-driven environment, which seeks punishment. In other words, it means to think differently after taking a closer look. It is not groveling, or begging or beating yourself up or showing super sorrow. This kind of performance is remorse, which is the result of being caught red-handed, which is driven by shame, guilt and the fear of punishment. Rather biblical repentance is a grace-filled, life changing moment that has nothing to do with punishment. Restoration is greater and sweeter than any judgment. It is the opportunity to intimacy with God and peace, and we get to experience how much God loves us. Mmmmmm!

Jesus came and revealed the full nature of His Father God (John 14:9–10). He was never angry with the prostitutes or the woman at the well who had five husbands or the corrupt tax collector named Zacchaeus. In the parable of prodigal son, the loving father overlooked his son's promiscuity and ran to embrace him. Jesus was only angry with the self-righteous, hard hearted, legalistic, judgmental scribes and Pharisees because they mishandled the statutes God had given them by turning them into a heartless legalism which burdened the earnest Jew to the point of hopelessness. He abhorred their hypocritical attitudes because they honored the letter of the law, and viciously distorted the spirit in which it was given (Mark 7:9–13). Jesus will always bring words of encouragement, never condemnation, it is usually other people or yourself who are quick tell you what is wrong with your life. God's ways are unique! The Holy Spirit will only convict you of righteousness; God never uses shame, fear or control to convict you. He changes you by convincing you of His love even in your weaknesses and sins. His love never changes, it never diminishes, it surrounds, it covers and it sustains you. The Gospel is the greatest love story ever told.

What about the words of Jesus when he said, John 16:8 "And when He (Holy Spirit) has come, He will convict the world of sin, and of righteousness, and of judgment." Jesus was not talking about the believer here, but the unbeliever who has neglected the truth and failed to believe in Him. Verse 9 shows clearly that Jesus is referring to those who do not believe. "Of sin, because they do not believe in Me." The Holy Spirit is at work bringing people to a place of decision and restoration. He is not convincing them of their sin but rather, convincing them that faith in Jesus is the answer to real life in this world and the next.

Experts have accused Christianity of putting guilt on people by criticizing their "sinful lifestyles." They say this causes depression, suicide and other adverse symptoms such as stress and/or fear. We have to drop the rocks because we know the answer to their woes—it is in a loving God who will not condemn, who offers mercy and grace to help in time of need. Real Christianity is not a guilt-ridden religion, but a relationship where the love of God motivates us. Unfortunately, many Christians can feel guilty when they think that they are not doing enough for God. They feel the yoke of religious duty—this is the result of finding their identity in what they do for God, instead of intimacy with God. The Lord God Almighty will love us better every time! That is the way it is! God loved us first (see 1 John 4:19) and we respond to His love and goodness toward us. It is never up to us because that puts us in the driver's seat and in our own wisdom, then we will end up driving ourselves into legalism.

So what is the solution for guilt? The cross of Jesus is the only antidote for sin's guilt. Immorality, failure, mistakes etc. cannot quench God's love because the source of this love is God Himself. His love for us compels us to change. Our ability to know, and feel this love has nothing to do with how we feel or what we have done, or how we have performed, it is everything to do with what God has done in regards to our worthiness. God sees us as worthy of His love, grace and mercy—it is as simple as that! Therefore, we have to see ourselves as worthy of His love. The bible tells us that we "*were* washed, we *were* sanctified, we *were* justified in the name of the Lord Jesus and by the Spirit of God" (1 Cor 6:11) and all this took place the moment we believed in Jesus.

Ephesians 3:19 says "to know the love of Christ which passes knowledge; that you may be filled with all the fullness of God." The great apostle Paul prayed for believers everywhere that they would *know* the love of Jesus that passes knowledge, which transcends the law, which surpasses every tradition, ritual, every feast day, every culture, and absolutely beyond any sin. If the love of God exceeds, transcends, outdoes, and surpasses knowledge, then it has to it is a matter of the heart, able to be experienced. This is a stunning truth, too marvelous for comprehension. It is any wonder that we stand in awe of Him!

Chapter 8

CULTURE CONFUSION

What God has done for us becomes a mysterious puzzle when the culture we live in is at odds with the truth of the bible, and is disguised, within an ingrained system of working for approval. In some cultures, men gain significance from physical strength and winning at all costs, where muscles and making money make the man! Also in many cultures, men do not have the freedom to show love. Their culture says is it a sign of weakness to express affection, but at the same time it seems it is acceptable to show anger, even to the point of wife beating. I have to say here that any culture that regards women as inferior and believes it is ok to use violence or oppress them in *any* way is far from God's best. If our culture does not line up with the life and teaching of Jesus Christ then the culture has to undergo thorough scrutiny. God's kingdom is about mercy, forgiveness, and unconditional love, gentleness, kindness, tenderness, and loyalty and these qualities are not just for the women!

In first century Israel, it was acceptable for men to kiss and embrace each other. Jesus said to Simon the Pharisee, "I came to your house and you didn't wash my feet. You didn't even greet me with a kiss. But this woman has not stopped kissing my feet" (see Luke 7:37–38). Kissing was a normal greeting. Remember

Judas betrayed Jesus with a kiss. In the parable of the prodigal son, when the father saw his son, he ran to him, and fell on him with compassion and in a loving embrace gave him a heartfelt kiss (Luke 15:20). In Rom 16:16, 1 Cor 16:20, 2 Cor 13:12, 1 Thess 5:26 and 1 Peter 5:14 Paul and Peter both encourage believers to greet one another with a holy kiss. In Acts 20:1 after an uproar, Paul called the disciples to himself, embraced them and departed. In verse 37 he is speaking to the Ephesian elders before his departure to Macedonia, he knelt down and prayed for them and they all wept freely, and fell on Paul's neck and kissed him.

Some boys learn that they must never cry in order to be a man and this has crept into the body of Christ. However, in both Old and New Testaments we find many male heroes who wept openly, who showed great emotion and who were obviously free to do so. In the book of Genesis, we read where Esau ran to meet Jacob, they embraced, kissed and wept together (33:4) and Joseph wept so loudly when he reunited with his brothers that the Egyptians and house of Pharaoh heard it (45:2). In Psalm 39:12, we learn that King David wept—"Hear my prayer, O LORD, and give ear to my cry; do not be silent at my tears; for I am a stranger with You, A sojourner, as all my fathers were." David was not ashamed to worship freely and demonstrably express his emotions and in 1 Samuel 20:41, when he learned that he had to flee from Saul and leave his covenant friend, and both he and Jonathan kissed one another, and wept together. The prophet Jeremiah was known as "the weeping prophet" (Jer 9:1)—he wept night and day lamenting for his people. In the New Testament, Jesus was not embarrassed to weep openly, to shed tears in public. He wept for his friend Lazarus (see John 11:35) and over Jerusalem because He knew people would perish there (see Luke 19:41). Hebrews 5:7 tells us that Jesus obtained our salvation through "loud crying and tears" when he agonized in the Garden of Gethsemane.

The apostle Paul suffered anguish of heart and cried many tears because of his love for the church at Corinth (see 2 Cor 2:4), and he wept as he admonished the Ephesians (see Acts 20:31). Why did we ever adopt the concept that real men don't cry or feel vulnerable? God did not make a mistake when he fearfully and wonderfully created men with tear ducts and emotions. God wants real people who are like His Son to reflect His gentleness, compassion and humility. God is an emotional God, not a heartless, stiff upper-lip deity who is unapproachable.

Some men have never experienced a father's love or all they have is the memory of a father's harsh discipline or even worse still the lack of their father's discipline. In some cultures, men do not feel a freedom to express sadness or express love openly to their children, and they have to have all the answers and be the stoic hero. However, no matter what culture you grew up in, no earthly father can fully reflect the perfection of God's love, which is unconditional. Jesus smashed the strict religious system of His society to fulfil and reveal that love—you are always on His mind and He is your biggest fan.

The Pharisees dropped their rocks when they saw the love of Jesus. Matthew and Zacchaeus completely turned around after an encounter with Him. A Jewish leader named Nicodemus came to Jesus to find out if he really was the Messiah. He came in the night because he was afraid of the other Pharisees (see John 3:20). He did not want his colleagues to know that he needed more than a stiff upper lip, heartless religion. Jesus told him the truth, that he needed to start life completely over again, leaving his old life behind. Many of us today are like Nicodemus, caring too much, about what our colleagues think. Jesus calls his sons to be bold and fearless, not proud and hard-hearted.

What does it take to be a man? The best place to look for the answer is in the life of Jesus. Most importantly, Jesus is God and He laid down His divinity and became a human man. When He walked the earth, He lived in a male dominated society where men sometimes had many wives. Women had very few human rights—they wore veils, and did the work of a servant. Rabbis refused to teach them, regarded them as ignorant and relegated them to the back seats of the synagogue, sometimes behind a screen or upstairs. However, Rabbi Jesus modelled a different type of manhood, one the world had never seen before—He stood up for the down trodden, He included women in ministry, and He held children in his arms and blessed them. He fearlessly rebuked the religious leaders who mistreated women and men, and He was not afraid to break with culture by having women friends like Mary, Martha as well as Mary Magdalene, who was previously a prostitute. He performed what no other rabbi would even dream of—He took the position of a slave and scrubbed dirty feet until they were clean and dried them with a towel (see John 13:5). He shocked his disciples by having a theological discussion with a Samaritan woman who I imagine had been constantly abused and no doubt her pain and torment was intolerable (see John 4:7–30). He healed a woman from an issue of blood, who was considered as an outcast, and in fact He praised her faith and He also praised a poor widow who only had one coin to give (see Mark 12:43). He allowed a woman who was a prostitute to touch Him by washing His feet with her tears and drying them with her hair and then praised her devotion and forgave her sin (see Luke 7:38, 47, 48). He raised a widow's son from the dead in a tiny village of Nain because he felt compassion for her. As a widow she was vulnerable and had no financial means to support herself and to make matters worse she would have been blamed for her husband's death and now for the son's death also (see Luke 7:1–16). In a male dominated culture, in front of angry men who were demanding death by stoning, He restored a woman caught in the act of adultery (see John 8). The world had never seen a man like this before. Jesus was a man to follow, imitate and exalt.

The Gospel writer Matthew was a tax collector for the Romans, who ignored his unethical behavior. Jesus found him in the midst of this dishonorable pursuit of wealth. To the eyes of the Jewish citizens, he was a traitor of the lowest kind. When Jesus saw Matthew sitting at the tax office in Capernaum, He said to him, "Follow Me." So Matthew arose and followed him" (Matt 9:9). What was Jesus thinking? When people encountered Matthew they would cross the street, he was an unclean outcast by his own doing! Matthew was used to demeaning comments, and looks of disdain, yet Jesus spoke to him, and welcomed him with a heart of understanding, humility and acceptance. Jesus actions were revolutionary, shocking and violated Jewish culture in the extreme. Jesus gave importance to a man in the margins of society. Matthew received an invitation to begin a new life. The same invitation is open to every man today. "Follow Me." Matthew stood up, left his corrupt takings behind and followed Jesus. You can too!

The thief on the cross, Nicodemus, Joseph of Arimathea, Zacchaeus and others all had personal, life changing encounters with rabbi Jesus. Zacchaeus was also a man who lived in the margins of society, like Matthew he was a corrupt tax collector, in fact he was more corrupt because he was a chief tax collector and he was rich (see Luke 19:2). He hired and fired people like Matthew and took a slice of their takings as well. Zacchaeus was desperate enough to forsake his pride and go out on a limb to catch a glimpse of Jesus and Jesus did not disappoint him. This may have been the first time Zacchaeus heard someone call him by his name, instead of a disparaging name. Jesus had no problem, with inviting himself to the home of a notorious sinner for dinner or attending a party thrown by another sinner–Matthew. Then an unexpected miracle happened "Zacchaeus stood and said to the Lord, "Look, Lord, I give half of my goods to the poor; and if I have taken anything from anyone by false accusation, I restore fourfold" (Luke 19:8). Zacchaeus in making restitution admitted he was a thief and all this in response to an encounter with the Lord Jesus, with truth and grace (see John 1:17). His life was never the same again.

These stories show us what it is to be a man with humility, power and compassion in any culture. Jesus related to men with an understanding and forthrightness that many men may not have experienced before. He modeled a different type of manhood to the way things were. When he walked the dusty roads, he treated everyone with respect, value and acceptance. The despised sinners, the outcasts, the lepers were ignored by many, but not in the eyes of Jesus.

Today in some parts of the world, girls must live in a culturally acceptable way, by gaining their significance by being a good housekeeper, mother and wife. Some in the church have grown up to believe that gender specific roles are normal, and there is pressure on them to conform to the expectations of what a woman's role is and when they are married they are validated by their husband's ministry. However, some of these dear women run into difficulties in pursuing their dreams because when nothing moves for them they make excuses by admitting that it is "not God's timing." Some women know that God has gifted them for leadership, and they feel powerless to see it come to pass in the church so the corporate world of business gets their best years. There are other Christian women who are academics and highly qualified in teaching, business and medicine and find their niche in the world where they are free to pursue their dreams. Is there something wrong with this picture? I have to say here that the Australian church generally promotes women in all areas of church ministry but it has not always been this way, even in my time. I firmly believe that all people have a profound purpose in God and if that purpose is domestic duties then those people deserve honor and validation.

What does it take to be a woman? The best place to look for the answer is the same for men and women—in the powerful, compassionate, and humble life of Jesus. Mary was a great part in the life of Jesus and yet to the world around her she was an adulterer. Nobody understood her, but regardless of what people thought she honored her "yes" and carried what God had placed inside of her to full term. Nevertheless she could not do this alone, God provided a man—Joseph who was willing to give up his life to see her fulfil her destiny. Joseph created a space for God to use a powerful woman and together they birthed the Savior. Do not forget that Joseph bore the brunt of marrying an unclean woman, a so-called sinner and overcome his cultural upbringing. Joseph defied his culture—he went against the status quo, married her and stood between her and the insults in order to protect what God was doing in Mary.

In Eph 6:5 and 1 Tim 6:1–2 Paul told slaves to obey and respect their Christian masters however, he never commanded those masters to free their slaves. Is Paul supporting slavery as many 19th century Americans argued? Verse 1 suggests that Paul was going along with the culture, the way things were so that God's name and His doctrine "may not be blasphemed." Rather, Paul challenged the attitudes of the culture in which slavery existed. Paul did not challenge the ungodly system of tax collection or the politics of Rome either. Nevertheless, the gospel does challenge culture. It challenges us to be fair in our dealings with people, to treat all people as equals, with honor and respect regardless of gender, ethnicity, skin color, education, or economic background. So how do we live in the midst of this conflict?

In some cultures it is acceptable to "greet one another with a holy kiss" (see Rom 16:16; 1 Peter 5:14). In other cultures, it is not appropriate. The symbolism of head coverings in the Corinthian church of the first century do not symbolize the same thing today. In some societies, head covering is a sign of submission or modesty (see 1 Cor 4:8–10), in others it is used as a prayer shawl. However, what is important to realize is that our new position in Christ is not dependent on the clothes we wear or how long or short our hair is. Paul instructions about head coverings was dealing with a cultural issue and he was encouraging Christians to show respect to those who felt the need to cover their heads. Fashions change from nation to nation, from one era to another and from one culture to another and from one century to another, only one thing is sure we have a choice and our salvation does not depend on fashion or the culture we live in. It is solely by faith in the suffering, death, resurrection, and ascension of the Lord Jesus Christ.

Paul told women in the Corinth that they were not permitted to speak in the churches, but to be submissive (see 1 Cor 14:34). This was a local problem associated with the culture in the Corinthian church and not a permanent policy because Paul had already said that he wanted all men and women to be ready to contribute with a "psalm, a teaching, a tongue, an interpretation or a revelation" (1 Cor 14:26). Our culture is definitely different to the culture of bible days, so many of the culturally determined policies of that day are no longer relevant. For example, Jesus chose Jewish twelve men to be apostles—does this imply that that all apostles must be men? Alternatively, was this Jesus being sensitive and honoring the culture of the Jewish people? In Jewish Law witnesses had to be men. The twelve had to be witnesses of the resurrection of Jesus (see Acts 1:22). It is possible to accommodate the culture around us without compromise, because we are witnesses in our community to both believers and non-believers. We have to remember that Scripture is the foundation for what we believe and what we do, not our culture. In all this culture confusion, we must never lose sight of the truth of how God sees us and what He has done for us.

The Apostle Peter had to change his deep-seated view of Jewish superiority and separatism after he received a vision from God recorded for us to read in the Book of Acts chapter 10. Peter shared his vision to a group of Gentiles who had gathered in the house of Simon the Tanner, He said, "You know how unlawful it is for a Jewish man to keep company with or go to one of another nation. But God has shown me that I should not call any man common or unclean" (Act 10:28). In verse 34, Peter said, "In truth I perceive that God shows no partiality." This would have been a bewildering admission for Peter because a Jewish man would begin every day with a prayer thanking God that he was not a slave, a Gentile, or a woman. Gentiles also despised Jews but all this changed right here with Peter's vision. First century Christians were the first people apart from Jesus to disregard racial prejudice and cultural limitations, and line up with the New Covenant of unearned grace, where we are all equal in Christ. It is interesting that Paul mentioned slaves, Gentiles and women in the same order when he wrote to the Galatians "There is neither Jew nor Greek, there is neither slave nor free, there is neither male nor female; for you are all one in Christ Jesus" (Gal 3:28). In addition, Jesus confronted the religious Jews who looked upon other races, as no better than dogs, we would call this racism today.

"He said to him, "What is written in the law? What is your reading of it?" So he answered and said, "'YOU SHALL LOVE THE LORD YOUR GOD WITH ALL YOUR HEART, WITH ALL YOUR SOUL, WITH ALL YOUR STRENGTH, AND WITH ALL YOUR MIND,' and 'YOUR NEIGHBOR AS YOURSELF.'" And He said to him, "You have answered rightly; do this and you will live." But he, wanting to justify himself, said to Jesus, "And who is my neighbor?" Then Jesus answered and said: "A certain man went down from Jerusalem to Jericho, and fell among thieves, who stripped him of his clothing, wounded him, and departed, leaving him half dead. Now by chance a certain priest came down that road. And when he saw him, he passed by on the other side. Likewise a Levite, when he arrived at the place, came and looked, and passed by on the other side. But a certain Samaritan, as he journeyed, came where he was. And when he saw him, he had compassion. So he went to him and bandaged his wounds, pouring on oil and wine; and he set him on his own animal, brought him to an inn, and took care of him. On the next day, when he departed, he took out two denarii, gave them to the innkeeper, and said to him, 'Take care of him; and whatever more you spend, when I come again, I will repay you.' So which of these three do you think was neighbor to him who fell among the thieves?" And he said, "He who showed mercy on him." Then Jesus said to him, "Go and do likewise" (Luke 10:26–37).

The Lawyer knew that Jesus had a reputation of being kind to people of other races and loving people who did not deserve it. He wanted to justify his strict law keeping, so he asked Jesus "Who is my neighbor?" In those days, let us face it—racism was alive and well between the Jews and the Samaritans, the Jews looked upon the Samaritans as religiously inferior and despised them, and the Samaritans hated the Jews. Therefore, to keep the peace they separated geographically and lived in segregation. In the parable, Jesus went straight to the lawyer's problem and challenged his bigotry.

Oh my, how shocking is this parable, these two religious men refused to help another human being who was dying. We are told a certain priest and a Levite both passed by on the other side, when it was very clear the man had been robbed and was half-dead. The Levite actually came close and looked at him, he would have seen his wounds, nakedness and the fact that he was still alive, then passed by on the other side and did nothing. Why? What were they afraid of? They were supposed to perform acts of mercy and they refused. I suggest they were afraid of breaking the rules, they valued their cultural preferences, and a strict adherence to the rules more than they valued another human life. This was religiosity in the extreme, considering the assaulted man was still alive.

By choosing a Samaritan for the part of a compassionate man, Jesus exposed their blatant intolerance for people of other races. Had the situation been reversed and the Samaritan was robbed and beaten to almost an inch of his life, the priest, the Levite and the lawyer, I suggest would not have come to the rescue. The opposite of racism or prejudice is so wonderfully represented in the actions of the Good Samaritan, and in the life of Jesus— compassion. Compassion forgets about self, and goes the extra mile! Compassion was the motivation for every interaction Jesus had with people.

I do not know any other way to say this, so I will let scripture speak for itself.

Col 2:20–23 TPT

> "For you were included in the death of Christ and have died with him to the religious system and powers of this world. Don't retreat back to being bullied by the standards and opinions of religion, for example, their strict requirements, "You can't associate with that person!" or "Don't eat that"" or, "you can't touch that!" These are the doctrines of men and corrupt customs that are worthless to help you spiritually. For though they may appear to possess the promise of wisdom in their submission to God through the deprivation of their physical bodies, it is actually nothing more than empty rules rooted in religious rituals!"[12]

Romans 12:2 TPT

> "Stop imitating the ideals and opinions of the culture around you, but be inwardly transformed by the Holy Spirit through a total reformation of how you think. This will empower you to discern God's will as you live a beautiful life, satisfying and perfect in His eyes."[13]

In other words, do not be conformed to the wrong customary beliefs of the society you belong to, rather let God and His Word change your thinking to line up with His ways. Living blindly by what the culture dictates without questioning it is too easy. Furthermore, it is too easy to live carelessly in a society where immorality is acceptable, without considering the consequences. It is too easy to follow unwritten traditions blindly when they insist we have to do the same things our parents and their parents have done, without thinking. It is plainly just too stupid to live by regulations and cultural restrictions that make many questionable behaviors acceptable. Kingdom culture should influence any culture because is not based on feelings, legalism or human philosophy—rather, it is based on Jesus Christ and His righteousness, peace, joy (see Rom 14:17), grace, truth, faith and so much more.

True Christianity is of the heart, it is a new birth, a new attitude, in Christ. More than half of Paul's life was a testimony to how religious laws, mixed with culture which were all devised by men did not work and he had no confidence in it!

Paul listed seven things in which he trusted–this is what religion/culture looks like.

1. He was circumcised on the eighth day
2. He boasted in his genealogy, he knew his pedigree
3. He was of the tribe of Benjamin; he belonged to the best family and boasted in it
4. He was a Hebrew of Hebrews; he was a leader in the highest religious circles
5. He was a proud Pharisee; he represented the very best in Israel
6. He thought he was doing God's will by persecuting the believers because they believed in their hearts and not in the law
7. He said he was blameless (see Rom 7:7), in other words he considered himself a super saint, because all the keeping of the law commended him to God

Then one day the whole thing changed, he met the Lord Jesus and suddenly it all became as rubbish and he no longer trusted in those things, now he trusted in the Lord Jesus and His righteousness through the cross (see Php 3:7–9).

Although it may often be hard to admit, we do base our lives and opinions on experiences with the culture we live in or the church in which we grew up. There comes a time when we realize that some of the things we learnt about our traditions or our culture was wrong. For example, I grew up believing that if I did not go to church every Sunday, I would go to hell, and that this was a mortal sin worthy of hell's fire. That is silly, it is completely the wrong motivation for attending church, and I just do not believe it anymore. Unfortunately, I have seen Christians be more outraged by a breach in their culture than a blatant misuse of God's Word. We are creatures of habit who tend to gravitate toward our own traditions. So then, we need to be sure that what we believe is scripturally correct and not based on our own traditional understanding of the way things were. The Berean Christians refused to take everything that the Apostle Paul preached at face value. They went home and studied the Scriptures to be sure that the things that Paul was saying were true (see Acts 17:11).

We have to ensure that we do not use our culture as a standard to measure scripture. We have to beware of the preaching that our ears want to hear, the preaching that belongs to the wisdom of the world. Paul wrote to the Corinthians and called the wisdom of this world foolishness (see 1 Cor 1:20). It is foolishness because the world does not know God and at the same time, it does not have the answers. We are not of the world, we belong to God; we were born again and transferred into the kingdom of the Son of God's love. In other words, we are separate from the world, now we live in fellowship with God because the loving Father has always been in fellowship with us. He loved us first; we have His guidance, comfort and protection all the time. God's heart towards us never changes, and His love is not determined by our behavior, but by His grace. 1 Cor 1:9 says, "God is faithful, by whom you were called into the fellowship of His Son, Jesus Christ our Lord." The Corinthians were not in fellowship with God because they were doing the right things, they were in fellowship because God first called them and He is faithful.

We love God because He first loved us. In everything in our Christian life, God is the initiator and we are the responders. It cannot be any other way because it is not up to us. We get to love God more and more with all our heart, soul, mind and strength (see Mark 12:30) because God first loved us, otherwise it becomes legalistic. He demonstrated His love by the work of Jesus on the cross—Jesus did all the work for us. His love for us has nothing to do with what we do or do not do. His love is unconditional and it is forever.

We have to be found in Him and see ourselves as God sees us, and it is all by faith (see Php 3:9). We have to see with the eyes of faith because we can't work for it, can't buy it, can't steal it, can't pretend it, can't look like it, can't act it out, can't perform for it and we can't do anything to earn it. We just have to know the truth so we can believe it, it is called trust, and it is for everyone who will accept it as truth.

If truth sets free, then lies imprison us. When you discover the truth then you don't have to believe the lie anymore. When you continually embrace grace and truth, it brings more freedom into your life; it brings lasting change/transformation on the inside by the Holy Spirit and the opinions of the culture you live in will not keep you bound. Transformation comes, by changing your mind about the wrong ideals you once believed and know the truth—the Lord of Life, who sets you completely free.

God needs men and women today who will faithfully pursue the call of God on their lives in the midst of cultural limitations. Jesus the most powerful person ever to walk the earth confounded the world by becoming a servant—He used His power to raise up those around Him rather than keep them in their place, He had no time for a culture that relegated people to an inferior status.

WOMEN ALSO WONDER WHAT GOD HAS DONE FOR THEM!

Galatians 3:28 says, "There is neither Jew nor Greek, there is neither slave nor free, there is neither male nor female; for you are all one in Christ Jesus." However, under the Old Covenant, men had more privileges; they alone had circumcision, which was the sign of the Covenant, they had the right to inheritances, they alone had the privilege of being kings and priests, etc. The good news—we are no longer under the Old Covenant, we are under a New Covenant where there is no distinction. We are all kings and priests unto God (see Rev 1:6). Earlier in the epistle, Paul wrote "O foolish Galatians! Who has bewitched you?" He had to remind them that life under the New Covenant is in Christ where we are all one. The dividing line between Jew and Greek was not the only dividing line erased.

When God said in Gen 2:18 "And the LORD God said, "It is not good that man should be alone; I will make him a helper comparable to him." He did not mean a house slave suitable for him for life. In the context of Genesis chapter two God is dealing with marriage and family, making the man's highest calling and greatest fulfillment—husband and father and a woman's highest calling—wife and mother. Christianity has traditionally held that the role of every female is solely to be a wife and mother and yet the highest calling for a man—to be a husband and father, is sometimes overlooked in the rush to promote men as pastors, leaders, decision makers, world changers and corporate ladder climbers.

Please understand here, I am not suggesting that marriage is for everyone, I am commenting on the passage. Being a wife, mother and grandmother is definitely my highest calling. Motherhood is clearly the hardest unpaid job in the world, which comes with utterly exhausting challenges, long hours, heartaches and rewards. These were the best days of my life—I learnt so much about myself, and my husband, about life and loving my children. Because I was a stay-at-home mom, I was able to do things that working moms never had the opportunity to do, but at the same time, the whole family had second hand everything. Unfortunately, however, it is my experience that stay-at-home motherhood is highly underrated, overlooked and sadly not valued equally compared to other professions, careers or callings. Today stay-at-home motherhood is not always a choice due to demanding financial pressures, and these families rely on grandparents and professional caregivers to fill the gap and the children turn out to be well-adjusted adults. The church for centuries has implied that working mothers neglect their children by pursuing a career. This mindset is irrational, to some degree demeaning and Scripture does not support it. It is a choice families are free to make. Christianity has also taught that the virtuous woman in Proverbs 31 was the model stay at home mom. That is not what the scripture says. She was an exceptional entrepreneur, a wise business woman, a creative garment maker, a real estate agent, a wine maker, an employer, as well as a mother and wife. Her work was not limited to the drudgery of housework. She ran her business from home and obviously did not stay there, and *may* even have employed others to look after her children.

Have you ever wondered why for centuries, the church taught that women should not work outside the home when the bible does not support it, nor does it place the burden of child-care solely on the wife! Nor does it suggest that she is naturally inferior. A quick look at bible commentaries gives us a clue. The following excerpts from John Gill 1697–1771 Bible Commentary are surely not what God had in mind when He created Eve as helper.

> "I will made him an help meet for him; one to help him in all the affairs of life, not only for the propagation of his species, but to provide things useful and comfortable for him; to dress his food, and take care of the affairs of the family; one "like himself" {c}, in nature, temper, and disposition, in form and shape; or one "as before him" {d}, that would be pleasing to his sight, and with whom he might delightfully converse, and be in all respects agreeable to him, and entirely answerable to his case and circumstances, his wants and wishes."

A commentary on Ephesians 5:22 by John Gill 1697-1771

> "Wives in obedience.; they should think well of their husbands, speak becomingly to them, and respectfully of them; the wife should take care of the family, and family affairs, according to the husband's will; should imitate him in what is good, and bear with that which is not so agreeable; she should not curiously inquire into his business, but leave the management of it to him; she should help and assist in caring and providing for the family; and

should abide with him in prosperity and adversity,
and do nothing without his will and consent."

Furthermore, a writer of the Apocrypha named Sirach, ignored the truth of shared responsibility for the sin of Adam and Eve and placed all the blame on Eve: "From a woman did sin originate, and because of her we all must die" (Ecclesiasticus (Sirach) 25:24). He also wrote, "Do not...sit in the midst of women; for from garments comes the moth, and from a woman comes woman's wickedness. Better is the wickedness of a man than a woman who does good; and it is a woman who brings shame and disgrace." (Ecclesiasticus (Sirach) 42:12-14).

Additionally, the rabbis of Jesus day denied women access to the Torah—"It is better that the words of the Law should be burned than that they should be given to a woman" (Sot. 3.4: 19a). "If a man gives his daughter a knowledge of the Law, it is as though he taught her lechery" (Sot. 4.3). Rabbi Jesus allowed Mary to sit at His feet and listen to what he said (see Luke 10:39) and Jesus did not put her in her place—the kitchen, rather He said that she had chosen the right place. "Only one thing is needed. Mary has chosen what is better, and it will not be taken away from her" (Luke10:42). By the way, Jesus never assigned domestic duties to women only—He washed feet and cooked fish. In Acts chapter 6 we read how seven men Stephen, Philip, Prochorus, Nicanor, Timon, Parmenas and Nicolas, a proselyte from Antioch were all of good reputation and full of the Holy Spirit and wisdom—were appointed to serve tables, clean up and wash dishes (see Acts 6:1–7).

Moreover, a church I attended in the nineties held the view that God designed women to serve their husbands, bear their children, and to submit and trust in their husband's decisions. Is it any wonder then that women in the church are screaming what has

God ever done for me? Is this all there is? God's wonderful, majestic and glorious vision for His daughters is far greater than being house bound and unable to make decisions for themselves. John Gottman, Ph. D, and Nan Silver write in their book The Seven Principles for Making Marriage Work, "Some men claim that religious conviction requires them to be in control of their marriages and, by extension, their wives. But there's no religion I know of that says a man should be a bully."[14]

If we use Paul's letter to the Christians of Ephesus, Corinth and Crete to declare the roles of men and women, and ignore the other six letters, then we have missed the mark resulting in restrictions on women, that God did not intend. We must be careful not to read into the bible something that is not there for example a misinterpretation of Titus 2:4-5 encompasses all women in the homemaker role, for as long as she lives.

Tit 2:4-5

> That they admonish the young women to love their husbands, to love their children, to be discreet, chaste, homemakers, good, obedient to their own husbands, that the word of God may not be blasphemed.

Paul wrote this letter to Titus who was a younger inexperienced minister to encourage him to pass on sound doctrine (see Tit 2:1–14). In Crete the people were famous for being lazy, drinking and immoral behavior (see Tit 1:12), and he did not want them to repeat the mistakes of their past idleness. Why? So "that the word of God may not be blasphemed." Paul was concerned that the believers by their behavior would jeopardize the spread of the gospel. In the same way, he was worried about head coverings in Corinth. He did not want the new Christians to offend the culture of the people there (see 1 Cor 10:31–33). He wanted the women to be good witnesses to their non-Christian neighbors by showing respect to husbands and being good homemakers. "Paul was not discouraging women from working outside the home because the concept of going to work was not an option for women in the first century. Paul's concern had nothing to do with women leaving their homes to pursue careers—because women in the agrarian society of Crete in the year 62AD did not do that! [15]

On a closer look in 1 Timothy 5, Paul was teaching the new converts to take their responsibilities as ministers, wives and mothers seriously. He also expressed his concern of the laziness of the women in Ephesus and instructed them to stay home and not waste time but look after their families properly (see 1 Timothy 5:13). In verse 14 he writes—"Therefore I desire that the younger widows marry, bear children, manage the house, give no opportunity to the adversary to speak reproachfully."[16]

In essence, Paul is saying that home life is important for both husband and wife, for every household, even for single moms and widows. We cannot use these verses to imply that all Christian women should be housekeepers, tending to the family all their lives and therefore ignore their God-given calling, gifts, talents and abilities outside the home. I do not know of any female who would not want to be a mother, but that should not prevent them from becoming teachers, nurses, doctors, lawyers, authors, business owners, or pastors, teachers of the Word, apostles, prophets, evangelists and so much more. God never intended these gifts to be restricted to men only. It should never be about roles but gifts. Roles lock women into the menial roles and men into the power roles. It has to be about gifts in the body of Christ because we are all one in Christ. For married couples—roles should be about mutual agreement about how they manage their child-care and housework. Just because a mother has a job does by not mean she is a poor mother.

I have attended Christian weddings where the minister has preached that it takes submissiveness, to be a great wife. This kind of preaching in the hearing of non-Christians gives the impression that those young wives are unable to make decisions and will only succeed as a good wife if she is retiring and compliant. This is not what the scripture says. Mary the mother of Jesus did not retire at the threat of being stoned to death, being shamed and labelled an adulteress, rather she determined to see it through, give birth to Jesus and save the world. Hannah a married woman, wept and prayed until a son came to her, in spite of being accused of being drunk, she spoke up for herself when Eli, the priest of the tabernacle, accused her of being drunk. "No sir!" Hannah replied. "I'm a deeply troubled woman. I've drunk neither wine nor beer. I've been pouring out my soul in the Lord's presence. Don't consider your maid servant a worthless woman. Rather all this time I've been speaking because I'm very anxious and distressed." "Go in peace," Eli answered. "May the God of Israel grant the request you have asked of him" (1 Sam 1:15–17). Initially Eli did not understand nor even recognize Hannah's burden or that it was the Spirit of God praying through her when she groaned in intercession, until she spoke up in determination and strength. Esther, a married woman, did not keep quiet when she rescued her nation from genocide. Also hidden in the Old Testament is the story of Zelophehad's daughters. They did not keep quiet when they approached Moses on the death of their father and put their case: "Why should the name of our father be withdrawn from among his family because he had no son? Give us possession among our father's brothers" (Num 27:4). These girls would have known that they had no rights, yet they stepped out bravely and challenged the leader of their nation, "So Moses brought their case before the LORD. And the LORD spoke to Moses, saying: "The daughters of Zelophehad speak what is right; you shall surely give them a possession of inheritance among their father's brothers, and cause the inheritance of their father to pass to them. And you shall speak to the children of Israel, saying: 'If a man dies and has no son, then you shall cause his inheritance to pass to his daughter" (Num 27:5-8). The daughters of Zelophehad asked Moses and Moses asked God and God in that moment, demonstrated that we are all equal in His Kingdom. The daughters took a stand because they knew they were not second best and deserved their share. Achsah was another who like Zeolophehad's daughters, also claimed land in Canaan (see Josh 14:13–19). In a time when women did not own anything, she not only asked for land but also for springs of water (v19). Caleb gave her the upper and lower springs and a blessing. She was her father's daughter and she was not going to live in the margins. Deborah, also a married woman was Israel's first and only female judge. Men and women came to her for judgement and she prophesied and told them what to do. She left her husband Lapidoth behind to look after the household because Barak insisted she go into battle and she did not flinch (see Judges 4). Jael an ordinary housewife, armed with a tent peg killed the enemy Sisera and put an end to the battle (Judges 5). God created Eve from Adam's side, named her after Himself (Helper—*ezer kenegdo*) and called her comparable or equal to Adam. She was 'bone of his bone and flesh of his flesh,' you cannot get closer than this as far as equal goes. She was to rule over creation beside Adam. God acknowledges the sheer strength, determination and bravery of many biblical women.

Jesus definition of submission is about giving from the life we have in Him, about mutual giving and receiving, standing against the forces that come against families together, this demands extraordinary commitment to tenacity, strength and courage. Making submission the operative word for women and not for men is asking for disaster. In The Seven Principles for Making Marriage Work, John M Gottman and Nan Silver, write—"For marriage to thrive, you have to share the driver's seat... In our long-term study of 130 newlywed couples, now in its eighth year, we have found that, even in the first few months of marriage, men who allow their wives to influence them have happier marriages and are less likely to divorce than men who resist their wives' influence. Statistically speaking, when a man is not willing to share power with his partner, there is an 81 percent chance that his marriage will self-destruct."[17]

God created his daughters to be helpers alongside his sons, not behind, underneath, or left back in the kitchen. Helper does not imply subservience or inferiority, and marriage is not a hierarchy! God's sons are to have Proverbs 31 daughters beside them, fully trusting each other, so there is no lack of profit. God's daughters do good and not evil towards the Proverbs 31 men all the days of their lives (see Prov 31:11, 12), their children rise up and called her blessed; her husband also, and he praises her (see Prov 31:29, 28). The whole family prospers because, God's daughter of valor (verse 10) fears the Lord (see verse 30), and she has a husband who supports her. The Proverbs 31 woman, who can find her today in the Church of Jesus Christ? Only where there is a Proverbs 31 man.

"Marriage works best when couples have need for each other and a sense of mutual dependence and shared authority. Children benefit when parents share authority, because there is a willingness to work together. The other kind of husband and father is a very sad story. He responds to the loss of male entitlement with righteous indignation or a sense of victimization. He may become more authoritarian or withdraw into a lonely shell, protecting what little he has left. He does not give others very much honor and respect because he is engaged in a search for honor and respect he thinks is his due. He will not accept his wife's influence because he fears any further loss of power and because he will not accept influence, he will not *have* very much influence. The consequence is that no one will much care about him while he lives nor mourn him when he dies."

The blueprint for marriage has to be mutual and voluntary submission one to the other out of reverence to Christ (Eph 5:21), because "Two cannot walk together unless they are agreed" (Amos 3:3), and because the two are one so one cannot be over or under the other one. True mutual submission is a trusting attitude voluntarily entered by both husband and wife where both have their needs met. "Acknowledging and respecting each other's deepest, most personal hopes and dreams is the key to saving and enriching a marriage." I have seen many happy, non-Christian marriages succeed and they are doing what comes naturally to them, voluntarily submitting to each other and working things out for the good of the family, and these couples have never read the bible. I have seen Christian marriages that are faithful but sadly dysfunctional, and I suggest it is because the wife blames the husband for every minor and every major problem because he is the head and therefore responsible. I have also seen a wife manipulate her husband to get what she wants by making him feel he makes the decision—he is happy because he thinks he is in control, and she is happy because she gets what she wants. This is not what God had in mind when He instituted holy matrimony. It is never right to manipulate or force a spouse to get what you want because they cannot act freely. Many successful Christian marriages uphold the headship of the husband and the submission of the wife teaching; however, they do not live it out in practice.

Most couples work together, each considering the other in all things. John Gottman Ph. D and Nan Silver write in their book The Seven Principles for Making Marriage Work, "Our research has included couples who believe the man should be the head of the family as well as couples who hold egalitarian viewpoints. In both kinds of marriages, emotionally intelligent husbands have figured out the one big thing: how to convey *honor and respect*. All spiritual views of life are consistent with loving and honoring your spouse. And that's what accepting influence is all about. After all, do you really want to make decisions that leave your wife feeling disrespected? Is *that* really consistent with religious beliefs? It is not."[18] Surely then if our lives and relationship with God do not line up with the life and teaching of the Lord Jesus then we need to take another serious look at our interpretation of Scripture.

Surely, only mutual and voluntary submission by both husband and wife creates a marriage that can withstand the tests that couples face. How can any marriage survive today in a culture where there is easy divorce, promiscuity and inequality? Only by putting God first in everything and trusting in Him. We have a wonderful model in Jesus and when we do life His way, we have a marriage that is sacrificial, has mutual submission, love and respect.

What did Jesus say about marriage?

Mat 19:3-10

> "And the Pharisees came to Him, tempting Him and saying to Him, Is it lawful for a man to put away his wife for every cause? And He answered and said to them, Have you not read that He who made them at the beginning "made them male and

female", and said, For this cause a man shall leave father and mother and shall cling to his wife, and the two of them shall be one flesh? Therefore they are no longer two, but one flesh. Therefore what God has joined together, let not man separate. They said to Him, Why did Moses then command to give a bill of divorce and to put her away? He said to them, Because of your hard-heartedness Moses allowed you to put away your wives; but from the beginning it was not so. And I say to you, Whoever shall put away his wife, except for fornication, and shall marry another, commits adultery; and whoever marries her who is put away commits adultery. His disciples said to Him, If this is the case of the man with his wife, it is not good to marry."

The Pharisees did not ask this question because they wanted an answer—it was in order to trap Jesus. They asked Jesus "Is it lawful for a man to put away his wife?" In today's world, this shocking question reveals a chauvinism of the worst kind to the point of misogyny. Herod put his wife away in order to marry his brother's wife, and when John the Baptist reproved him Herod imprisoned him and eventually beheaded him. I am reminded of the poem—King Henry VIII, to six wives he was wedded. One died, one survived, two divorced, two beheaded."[19]

Jesus turned this trap into an equality issue, by referring back to the Garden before the fall of Adam. He reminded them of God's ultimate design for man and woman in marriage. "No longer two, but one flesh, therefore what God has joined together, let not man separate (verse 6), and if they marry someone else, they commit adultery" (verse 9). He was saying that their wives were their equal, not their possessions to be divorced because they burned the biscuits. God's divine plan was for husband and wife for life where a man leaves his father's influence and clings to his wife. This was a shocking thought for the Pharisees of Jesus' day, as their culture dictated that a wife had to leave her parents and be absorbed into her husband's family. Even the disciples many of whom were married, had difficulty, they had never heard such a radical view of marriage, they said, "If this is the case of the man with his wife, it is not good to marry." Jesus answered them by reminding them that Moses permitted divorce because of the hardness of their heart but from the beginning, God ruled that the man was to cleave to his wife because the two were one flesh, joined by God himself and to remain so. "Marriage is a sacred design of an Almighty God and it merges the man and the woman so that they are one again."[20]

Is the Gospel good news for women and girls? Does the gospel, the Good News of the Lord Jesus Christ the church preaches today open the door for women and girls to be equal contributors to the Body of Christ? It is ridiculous that I should even ask this question, the gospel is surely big enough for all of us to be involved in every capacity regardless of gender. In my travels mostly in Asia, I visit churches on a Sunday when I can, and there are significantly more women. However, in some of these churches I personally know that the women are restricted from active participation in ministry. There was a time, in my life when I threw my bible down in frustration, knowing what God had for me but because of culture and bias, never fully experiencing it. Unfortunately, when I purchased an ereader I could not throw it anymore, so I had to be content knowing what God had done for me and knowing that all I had to do was keep on studying and stay faithful to the challenge. I know I am not the only one, who has felt this way, many women wonder what God has for them and what is the meaning of "Where the spirit of the Lord is there is liberty" (see 2 Cor 3:17). Others wonder if there is something inherently wrong with them because of their gender and unfortunately, their Christianity is sometimes up and down, spiritually high one minute and doubting the next, and sometimes they will even turn away from God or throw their bible at the wall. Is it any wonder leadership think women are not good leaders, and relegate them to the pews!

When the Holy Spirit fell on the 120 in the upper room, the church was born, and anointed for ministry. This anointing poured out on men and women, without bias, and Peter announced that all would be empowered to preach the gospel. The Holy Spirit came and broke the barriers of race, culture, age, gender and economic class. He came to empower us all, nowhere in the Word of God does it endorse the idea that women are inferior or that spiritual gifts and callings are for males only. The Great Commission is not a men only affair. We need each other desperately!

Many Churches today are releasing women to minister outside of women's meetings, the family and the kitchen. The Christian life is not just about a personal relationship with God; every single one of us is to co-labor with God, to do the work of the ministry, and this could be in the kitchen, and in the family for both men and women. All Christians are equipped to be witnesses (see Acts 1:8).

Can I say here that when we compartmentalize women whose husbands are unsaved, or women who are single, childless, or divorced, we unwittingly limit the Holy Spirit! God never intended for men and women to derive their worth from what they do, or who their husband is. Who we are is in Christ only. We are complete in Him. Col 2:10 says, "You are complete in Him, who is the head of all principality and power." This goes for all of us, we are all God's image bearers and His sons and daughters (see Gal 3:26-28).

Chapter 10

THE OLD IS OUT!

We have to wake ourselves up sometimes and give ourselves a good talking to because we forget God's wonderful love for us or we have no knowledge of God and what He has done for us. The Corinthians, the Galatians, Michael and Arthur did not understand the freedom and liberty of the Holy Spirit. They did not know what God had done for them, because some false teachers had confused and twisted the truth. Have you noticed that many of Paul's writings deal with false teachings about the unearned gift of the righteousness of God?

Very briefly—the Books of Romans speaks about righteousness and justification through faith alone. First Corinthians speaks about the Christian living in grace and God's righteousness. Second Corinthians is to instruct about true ministry and the grace to give. Galatians speaks of freedom from the guilt trip of the law and justification through faith alone. Ephesians speaks of who the believer is in Christ. Philippians writes about the joy of freedom. Colossians is freedom from the law. First Thessalonians confirms disciples in the fundamental truths of the gospel. Second Thessalonians is urging believers to stand fast in the truth. First Timothy is against legalism and false doctrines. Second Timothy brings to light salvation through His finished work. Titus speaks of the light of salvation and has instructions on sound doctrine. Philemon speaks of abundant forgiveness and complete restoration. The Book of Hebrews speaks of Jesus Christ as God and The Great High Priest. It speaks of the law ending in the New Covenant in His redeeming Blood. All the general epistles in some way also warn about the divisiveness and dangers of false teachers who were infiltrating the Body of Christ. James gives us practical truths about what it means to be declared righteous by God and justification by faith, not works. First Peter mentions God's overcoming gift of grace and salvation through the cross of Jesus. First John speaks against false teachers and reminds the reader that the blood of Jesus cleanses us from sin. Second John warned the church to be aware of itinerant false teachers. Third letter of John mentions divisiveness within the church. Attention please—the old is out!

Clearly then the first century Christians had difficulty accepting the free gift of grace, because of the culture they had grown up in. They had difficulty accepting the fact that salvation was unearned, unmerited, that the righteousness of God, forever forgiveness and freedom in the Holy Spirit was freely given and available for everyone, without exception. For many Christians today the same difficulty still exists.

Chapter 11

EVERY SIN IS FOREVER FORGIVEN AND TAKEN AWAY

No more wondering what God has done for you! You don't have to be forever foggy about your forgiveness. Of all the many things God has done, this has to be the biggest, because it restored fellowship with our loving Father by making everything right again. Scripture clearly says that because of the blood of Jesus, forgiveness of *all* our sin was accomplished (see Col 2:13b), for all who would believe it, and it is forever. When Jesus died on the cross; we were not even thought of so all our sins were in the future and they were *all* forgiven in one event—it was a once and for all occasion. How can this be? God took all our sins, even the ones in the future, He put them on Jesus, when he was hanging on the cross, judged them, and Jesus paid the penalty for us. It is a done deal! We will never ever be liable for our sins ever again, even the ones we have not committed yet. It is the gift of righteousness. 2 Cor 5:21 says, "For He made Him who knew no sin to be sin for us, that we might become the righteousness of God in Him."

But wait there is more! Jesus not only took our punishment, in addition, He removed our sin from us, as far as east is from west (see Psalm 103:12). John the Baptist made the announcement at the beginning of Jesus' public ministry, "Behold the Lamb of God who takes away the sin of the world" (John 1:29). The blood of the sacrificial lamb in the Old Testament could not take sin away, it was powerless to deal with the worshipper's conscience (see Heb 9:9), and it required daily, weekly, monthly and yearly sacrifices (see Heb 10:11-12, 14). When the blood of an innocent animal was sprinkled on the Mercy Seat, on the Day of Atonement, sins were considered covered by the blood. It was a temporary fix until the New Covenant in the blood of Jesus—the innocent Lamb of God who would accomplish far more than an innocent animal. His shed blood would take sins away completely (see Heb 9:23). John the apostle wrote, "You know that He was manifested to take away our sins, and in Him there is no sin" (1 John 3:5). Under this New Covenant God writes on our hearts, and promises to remember our sins no more.

> "For this is the covenant that I will make with the house of Israel after those days, says the Lord: I will put my laws in their mind and write them on their hearts; and I will be their God and they shall be my people.... For I will be merciful to their unrighteousness, and their sins and their lawless deeds I will remember no more" (Hebrews 8:10, 12).

There it is—"God has forgiven all unrighteousness, sin and lawless deeds and will remember them no more." Jesus actually defined the New Covenant when He said, "For this is My blood of the new covenant, which is shed for many for the remission of sins" (see Mat 26:28). The blood of Jesus obliterated the record of sin when Jesus cried out, "It is finished!" When Jesus died on the cross as a substitute, He did not just cover our sin, He took them away, forever, and God will not remember them. Hebrews 9:26 says, "He then would have had to suffer often since the foundation of the world; but now, once at the end of the ages, He has appeared to put away sin by the sacrifice of Himself." Jesus destroyed, did away with, and blotted out every sin. It is just as if we have never sinned, but it is more than that. God is not just overlooking our sins, they are not just forgiven—they are gone, taken away, obliterated, and destroyed. Taken away from us and forgiven.

To get your head around this mind-blowing truth you have to understand that Jesus was sinless so He was the only one who would pay for all the sins of everyone. Jesus is the only way to the Father, there is no other way. Jesus dealt with everyone's sin on their behalf means that everyone needs to deal with Jesus personally. Either accept or reject Him. There is no salvation without Him and it is all by grace through faith. No one deserves it—it is a gift (see Romans 5:18-19). Righteousness is not about us doing right it is about what Jesus did for us and there is no sin which is not forgiven (see Col 2:13-14).

Now we have the Holy Spirit and grace to empower us to overcome any sin. The gospel really is good news! If we have missed understanding this truth, we will always wonder what God has done for us. We also need to understand deep in our hearts that God will never punish us with sickness, diseases, tragedies, weather events or accidents for our sins. Psalm 103:4 says, "Who redeems our lives from destruction, and crowns us with lovingkindness and tender mercies." Instead, we look to Jesus on the cross and receive wholeness from Him.

So now, when God looks at us He sees us righteous and just as if we had never sinned because we are fully and freely forgiven forever and our sins are gone for good! Here is the truth, the whole truth and nothing but the truth—Jesus is the truth and He has set us free from the power of sin over our lives. "Now we can draw near to God with a true heart in full assurance of faith, having our hearts sprinkled from an evil conscience and our bodies washed with pure water" (Heb 10:22).

Chapter 12

WHAT IS TRUTH?

Without beating around the bush, the truth is we have all inherited beliefs that do not line up with the truth of God's Word. Our problem is that we don't care or have the time to read the truth for ourselves, so we will go with the status quo. Therefore, it must be right! Right? When and if we do look for the truth we find that it was right after all, the bible says it so it must be right. However, on a closer look we find that the quote was out of the context of the chapter, and even the whole bible. For example, for many years Christian slaveholders in America used the bible to justify slavery. They even fought to keep slaves, partly for selfish economic reasons and partly because they wrongly believed the bible gave them the right to enslave people (see Colossians 3:22, 4:1). However, there were Christians who also used biblical principles to fight against slavery.

This verse from the bible - "And you shall know the truth and the truth shall set you free" (John 8:32), has been misquoted in all kinds of literature, for example—James A Garfield Quotes "The truth will set you free, but first it will make you miserable."[21] What is the truth that Jesus was talking about, and who was Jesus talking to when he said this? Here is the scripture—

"Then Jesus said to those Jews who believed Him, "If you abide in My word, you are My disciples indeed, and you shall know the truth, and the truth shall make you free." They answered Him, "We are Abraham's descendants, and have never been in bondage to anyone. How can You say, 'You will be made free'?" Jesus answered them, "Most assuredly, I say to you, whoever commits sin is a slave of sin. And a slave does not abide in the house forever, but a son abides forever. Therefore if the Son makes you free, you shall be free indeed. I know that you are Abraham's descendants, but you seek to kill Me, because My word has no place in you. I speak what I have seen with My Father, and you do what you have seen with your father" (John 8:31–38).

Jesus was talking to the Jews, who believed in Him, and they grew up committing to memory the whole Mosaic Law and trying to obey it, which was not only impossible but brought fear and guilt when they failed. Just knowing the scripture will not set you free, Jesus told the Pharisees in John 5:39–40 "You search the Scriptures, for in them you think you have eternal life; and these are they which testify of Me. But you are not willing to come to Me that you may have life." Obviously just knowing scripture is not the answer. The answer is in knowing Jesus. He is our source, our Savior, life-giver and there is none like Him. The ultimate truth of the bible is the Lord Jesus Christ—He said, "I am the way, the truth and the life" (see John 14:6). Jesus is the one who set us free, knowing Him firsthand and encountering Him on a personal basis transforms us and sets us free from the slavery to sin, and self-imposed limitations. The truth alone will not set you free but an intimate knowledge of the Truth—Jesus, will.

Jesus said "If you abide in My word, you are My disciples indeed" (verse 31). Disciples are learners, they live to know the truth, then Jesus said, "And you shall know the truth, and the truth shall make you free." So Jesus was saying, in other words, "Knowing me will make you free, there is no freedom in memorizing and keeping the law." The bible says in John 1:17 "For the law was given through Moses, but grace and truth came through Jesus Christ." The Law was *given,* but grace and truth *came* in Jesus. Grace has a face—Jesus! That is why you cannot mix the law and grace.

Then the next question we ask is what does keeping the law mean and why is there no freedom in it? It is impossible for a human being for their whole life to keep the Ten Commandments, even if we are the best person in the world at some point we will slip, and then we feel guilty and worry about the punishment, so where is the freedom in that? There is no freedom when fear has a foothold.

Jesus established a New Covenant (see Heb 8:13) based entirely on justification by faith, that is by believing in His finished work on the cross (see Acts 13:38–39), not by keeping the Ten Commandments (see Rom 10:4). Jesus did what the Ten Commandments could not do for us. All the law can do now, is expose our sin, and tell us when we fail, it cannot cover, cleanse, make us righteous, holy or remove sins. Only the Blood of Jesus can do that, and it is all by grace through faith not by works. Jesus fulfilled all that the Old Covenant of Law could not achieve by instituting a New and better Covenant thus making the Old obsolete (see Heb 8:6, 13). Now that has to be Good News! Right?

For some people it feels good to be able to do something to make it right by doing penance, because the punishment becomes the pill that eases their guilt. The truth is that having chosen to accept Jesus and know His truth, we are forgiven (see Col 2:13), and having experienced being unconditionally loved by God, we are free to go and sin no more, without guilt and fear of punishment if we fail. God's love for us is unfathomably greater than our sin; this incomprehensible love alone casts out the fear of punishment, overtakes us, cascades over us and drives the fear of punishment far from our hearts. Take a moment to read this verse thoughtfully from The Passion Translation 1 John 4:18–19 says, "Love never brings fear, for fear is always related to punishment. But love's perfection drives the fear of punishment far from our hearts. Whoever walks constantly afraid of punishment has not reached love's perfection. Our love for others is our grateful response to the love God first demonstrated to us."

God's love for us has to be the motivating factor in our relationship with Him. We love Him because He first loved us (1 John 4:19). When we allow His love and acceptance to wash over us, then we know the truth and know that we are free to love Him. Then we have unlimited grace, hope and faith to see us through anything. I am talking about anything, and everything! The truth about God's love for us always sets our heart free, free from ourselves, free from sin, bad habits, free from religious duty and the guilt and punishment that goes with it. Always remember the Father loved us first!

The Father in the Prodigal Son story in Luke 15 did not punish his immoral, selfish and rebellious son instead; he fell upon his son with an embrace, kissed him even though he smelt like a pigpen. He lavished him with love, acceptance and the robe of righteousness, the signet ring of authority and put sandals of right standing on his feet. There was no condemnation or punishment at all, just love, mercy, grace, acceptance and an unconditional welcome home son and the son did not even get to confess his rebellion. Did he deserve this treatment? No! This is the Father's love and underserved grace at work and it is available for you.

Here is the truth we can all be free from the pain and the guilt of the past. The answer is not in works, or trying harder it is in the Son of God—"Casting all your care upon Him, for He cares for you" (1 Peter 5:7). By knowing that you are accepted in Jesus, that you are righteous through Him, and knowing that in God's eyes you are washed clean and excessively and unconditionally loved by Him, you are set free to be the person God created you to be. The answers are in Jesus and what he achieved for you at the cross and that is the truth that sets you free! Can you hear me clapping?

We should all be theologians in the true sense of the word, and diligently search out the scriptures for ourselves. Heaven's freedom is available to every believer; we all need to take a closer look at God. We need to find answers to questions like do I really matter to God?" Does God really care about what is happening? We are to run the race God has "marked out for us" (see Heb 12:1-2). How do we know which race to run? By understanding that it is not determined by our gender, status, ethnicity or how much money we have or do not have! He is at work on our behalf, His plans are for our good, and He will complete it.

We all have regrets, if we had only done it this way or that way, if only we did not miss that opportunity, if only this person had not interfered, if only, if only… Some people think that it is the prejudices of other people that are holding them back and in some situations, this may be so, but the truth is we are all born again children of God, made in His image, where everyone is equally superior, and this truth alone should be enough for us to be content in any situation. God never intended for there to be inequality between races or gender and Christians should not hold an opinion that is different to God's view. I know this for sure none of us are called to sit on sideline or play 'left back at home' or just be the faithful supporter or spectator, or a church pew sitter—black, white or yellow skinned, male or female we are all to be active players and run the race He has marked out for us. His plans for His people are unique—He does not use the same plan for everyone, and it is not over until it is over. Romans 8:28 says "And we know that all things work together for good to those who love God, to those who are the called according to His purpose." Knowing and understanding God's sovereignty, can transform us. Someone shout AMEN!

Chapter 13

TRADITION

There is nothing wrong with having traditions; however, they can become a serious problem if they hinder people from a personal relationship with God through the work of Jesus on the cross. They become a burden hard to bear if they replace the Gospel of Grace. Traditions can stop the flow of grace in the life of a believer and have great potential to foster an atmosphere of superiority and control over people, which belongs to God alone. Traditions can also keep people in the dark about what God has done for them because the meaning behind the tradition can be lost in the maze of symbolic ritual.

In the period between the Testaments, the rabbis and religious leaders added their own interpretations and by Jesus day, their traditions had taken a prominent place alongside scripture. Jesus said in Mark 7:8-9 "For laying aside the commandment of God, you hold the tradition of men—the washing of pitchers and cups, and many other such things you do." He said to them, "All too well you reject the commandment of God, that you may keep your tradition."

The Rabbis teaching derived authority from tradition, and they labored in the study of the Mosaic Law. The Scribes were the exponents of the traditional law and those laws put heavy burdens on people but they never initiated any effort to remove those burdens. Learning and exclusiveness of knowledge had become their way of life, but it hindered and robbed the people from knowing God and what He had done for them (see Luke 11:37–54). However, Rabbi Jesus accurately taught what He had received from the highest authority. His teaching was not man's invention, or from tedious study of the Law—He received it by abiding in His Father, and He spoke it with authority. Jesus said in Matt 11:28–30 "Come to Me, all you who labor and are heavy laden, and I will give you rest. Take My yoke upon you and learn from Me, for I am gentle and lowly in heart, and you will find rest for your souls. For My yoke is easy and My burden is light." The rest that Jesus gives is a gift it is unearned and unmerited and it focuses on Him and not on our efforts, traditions, or where we sit in church every Sunday. It is never about us! It is about Jesus and His sacrifice. It is not about us reaching up to Him it is about God moved by compassion and mercy, reaching down to us and providing a salvation we could never accomplish. That alone is the reason for our worship, praise, adoration, commitment and that is why His yoke is easy and His burden is light.

Our hearts can be stone cold, like the Pharisees, and distracted by our traditions because we have always done it this way. We can accumulate a lot of knowledge about God and our traditions and miss knowing the One of whom it is all about. Jesus is the Bread of Life, He is real food for our souls, He is the lover of our souls, and we cannot do Christianity without an intimate heart knowledge of Him.

Chapter 14

MISREPRESENTING GOD

When Christians misrepresent God, the message it sends is that God is unjust. Jesus hated the distortions of His Father's word; it was the misrepresentations of the Pharisees that triggered his anger. Those who taught it were the self-declared righteous who despised and looked down on others. In contrast, Jesus friends were fishermen, corrupt tax collectors, prostitutes, sinners and the unclean etc. He shared meals with them, He healed them, He accepted everyone who came to Him, He raised people from the dead, He taught in the public places so women could learn, and he never excluded anyone. In a synagogue on the Sabbath day, He healed a woman who could not stand upright. Jesus was a counter-cultural radical man who challenged their traditions, because they had lost the true meaning and had become ritualistic.

He belittled the religious leaders of His day, by calling them "blind guides," "fools," "brood of vipers," "hypocrites," "whitewashed tombs," yet in spite of this He responded to their questions. Why was Jesus so hard on the Pharisees? Because the Pharisees were the ones who handled the Word of God and taught the people, they were the experts. He called them hypocrites because their traditions overlooked the love of God. Jesus warned them about doing good works for appearances sake and how fasting loses its value when it is from a wrong motivation (see Matt 6:16–18). He saw their elitism and their 'righteous tradition' of not associating with sinners as a pride-filled hypocritical barrier to His Kingdom coming on earth as it is in Heaven. He challenged the teaching that demanded the Jews separate themselves from sinners and Gentiles by healing a Canaanite woman's daughter, asking for a drink from a Samaritan woman, telling the parable of the Good Samaritan, and preaching that they should love their neighbors as themselves. He confronted their sense of superiority by telling the story of the Pharisee and the Tax Collector (see Luke 18:9–14). He declared that they were void of understanding (see Matt 12:1–8), He accused them of blatant transgression (see Matt 15:3). He pronounced woes on them (see Matt 23:1–36). At no point did Jesus compromise the Law of Moses. Rather he verbally attacked the Scribes and Pharisees who zealously protected their traditions, which did not reveal the heart of God.

Jesus was not against the Law, he was against legalism and the traditions of men; He reinterpreted it by challenging their understanding of the Law and even added a new dimension (see Matt 5:17–20). He showed them true righteousness that had everything to do with the heart. He said things like "You have heard it said… but I say to you (see Matt 5:21, 48). He said things like murder, and adultery begin in the heart, marriage is sacred and binding, and love your enemies (see Matt 5:20–48). He opposed their view of women by putting them in the spotlight. The first person He appeared to after His resurrection was Mary Magdalene and women were the first to find the empty tomb and the first to hear His command to go and tell (see John 20:17; Luke 24:9). He openly defied the concept the Pharisees had about the Sabbath being used to limit people, and weigh them down by defining what work could and couldn't be done, or how many steps one could walk (see Matt 12:8–12), which was focused on doing and not on God. The establishment of the original Sabbath was to remember who God is and what He has done.

When Christians do not understand the fullness of God's promises, and therefore do not really understand what God has done—you can be sure it because of lack of knowledge. Just like children who are afraid of spiders, just because they look scary but if they knew, more about them that fear would vanish. You can also be sure that the devil has a hand in it; his strategy is to put controversy around powerful truths.

Chapter 15

POLITICS, POWER AND POPULARITY

In John 11:47–50 we see a picture of how insidious the operation of legalism, power, pride and fear is in hiding the truth of what God has done for us. "Then the chief priests and the Pharisees gathered a council and said, "What shall we do? For this Man works many signs. If we let Him alone like this, everyone will believe in Him, and the Romans will come and take away both our place and nation." And one of them, Caiaphas, being high priest that year, said to them, "You know nothing at all, nor do you consider that it is expedient for us that one man should die for the people, and not that the whole nation should perish."

The chief priests who were largely Sadducees at that time and the Pharisees saw the many miracles Jesus did; there was no lack of evidence. What a scheming, power hungry group of men! The two parties were opposed to each other yet they joined in a common hatred to stop the uprising in the things of God by hatching a scheme to get rid of the troublemaker. If they could stop Jesus, their control, domination and manipulation of the people could continue and their need for power would be satisfied. They were driven by fear—fear of Rome's criticism and fear of the nation turning to Jesus and against them, which would bring a reformation of their carefully laid structures. They reasoned that the best thing would be if Jesus died at the hand of Rome, they would be blameless, and so the scheming began.

The Scripture goes on to say in John 11:53 "Then, from that day on, they plotted to put Him to death. Therefore Jesus no longer walked openly among the Jews, but went from there into the country near the wilderness, to a city called Ephraim, and there remained with His disciples." This then was probably the end of Jesus public ministry as the Gospel of John moves on to the last week of the earthly life of Jesus. My point here is that there is always a danger of adding to or taking away from the gospel when pride, power, popularity and fear are factors.

Chapter 16

GOD IS SO GOOD!

Legalism does not want you to know that God is good. It says that God is good, all the time, but then blames Him for murderous terrorist attacks and devastating natural disasters then use the bible to back up their claim.[22] Others will write it off by saying that "God works in mysterious ways." Please understand me here, people can say whatever they like and this is exactly what I am doing writing this book and you do not have to agree with me. However, when God is blamed for destruction or is called out for allowing bad things to happen, I get angry because it is simply not true! It is inconsistent to say that God is good and then say He performs evil to teach us a lesson or to demonstrate His wrath at the sinful ways of a nation. It is an oxymoron to say that God is good and then preach that devastation and disasters are "acts of God," or that bush fires, tsunamis, volcanic eruptions and earthquakes and are sent by God to deal with our pride, prejudices and sinfulness.[23] This is a distorted view of God, a misrepresentation of who God really is.

Furthermore, blaming God for devastating tragedies creates confusion in discerning what is from God and what is not? If God makes people sick to teach them something then why do we ask God to make them better? If droughts and bush fires are the judgments of an angry God sent to punish us, then how do we explain the heart-breaking destruction, loss of life and property, and why do we pray for rain and spend hundreds of exhausting hours attempting to douse the flames? This mind set can lead to thinking that everything comes from God and that there is no devil. Jesus said in John 10:10 "The thief does not come except to steal, and to kill, and to destroy. I have come that they may have life, and that they may have it more abundantly." Clearly then our enemy is a thief who kills and destroys and Jesus gives abundant life. One is bad the other is good. Jesus is the Good Shepherd who lays down His life for His sheep (see John 10:15). Jesus came to destroy the works of the devil (see 1 John 3:8), He came to reveal the goodness and mercy of a loving Father, He put a face to grace and mercy and declared the acceptable year of God's unmerited, unearned, undeserved favor. We have to test everything against the bible and the life and teachings of the Lord Jesus Christ. The devil is a liar, a deceiver, a thief, a murderer and a destroyer and he is free to operate only when Christians believe his obvious lies. "Oh, taste and see that the LORD is good; blessed is the man who trusts in Him!" (Psalm 34:8).

Chapter 17

WHAT ARE WE AFRAID OF?

When Jesus walked the earth, the Pharisees were famous for being afraid of sin and so invented many rules to keep everybody under control, and if the rules were broken, there were punishments. The fear of punishment ruled their lives and shaped their culture. Jesus on the other hand, had friends who were famous for breaking the rules and Jesus was not afraid of it. Rather His love led people and empowered them to rise above their mistakes and issues. The Pharisees were afraid of losing their control of the people. I hope you are recognizing the tactics the enemy has used throughout church history in an effort to prevent believers from having access to the most powerful truths in God's Word. Yes, we have an enemy and he has been defeated, however, he is a liar and a deceitful thief and does not deserve our attention at all. We have to test his lies against the Scriptures and base what we believe on the Word of God. There is no rule in the bible to say we cannot study/read the Word of God for ourselves.

What are we afraid of? Finding a loving Father, who is ever ready to love us better with an embrace? A Father who has promised to forget our sin, and never, ever punish us or leave us? For too long the people of God have heard that keeping the Ten Commandments, produces holiness, but this is a lie because the power to overcome sin is in a loving, Father by grace through faith. It is time to see that the only one who benefits from this is the enemy, and he has not rights at all.

At the outset of His ministry Jesus announced that he had come to set the oppressed free (see Luke 4:18). He came to a people burdened by rabbinic rules and regulations, which placed them under submission to the letter of the law. A world where legalism prevailed and was all that mattered. A world where leaders valued the traditions more highly than the meaning behind them (see Mark 7:5–8). A world where the ordinary Jew felt that every moment he was in danger of transgressing the law and the sinner had no hope at all. So Jesus did not come to make life better for the people, He came to change it completely, from an Old Covenant by the blood of a lamb to a New Covenant in His blood.

What are we afraid of? A life without rules to keep us in check? Are we afraid of a new life without guilt, condemnation and shame? Are we afraid that we actually *can* come to God freely, without having to belittle ourselves and beg for mercy? The truth is we come on the foundation that we are His sons and daughters! We confess that we messed up because we really did not understand how much He loves us. There is nothing to be afraid of, nothing at all! Just come!

Chapter 18

HYPOCRISY

Israel had been blessed by God to be a blessing (see Genesis 12), but when the exponents of the Law took the blessings and turned them into curses, the Son of God objected. Jesus was no wimp—He reinterpreted the Law and their traditions for them according to the Spirit in which Father God intended. When Jesus was confronted with bigotry and hypocrisy he was angered—He made a whip of cords, and drove the money changers out of the temple, along with the sheep and the oxen, and spilled the changers' money and overturned the tables and the seats of those who sold doves (see John 2:15, Matt 21:12, Mark 11:15). This was the radical, indignant, and deep-seated action of a man, motivated by His Father's love for ordinary people, who were being hard-done by in the House of God.

At another time the Pharisees insulted the parentage of Jesus by accusing Him of being born of fornication (see John 8:41). How did Jesus react? Read it for yourself it is a very skillful reply (John 8:39–59). In short, Jesus named the devil as the deceiver and He openly shared His insight that the devil was their father because there was no truth in their words and they pretended to be godly, when in reality their lives were far from it. Jesus asked two questions firstly, "Which of you convicts me of sin? Secondly, "I tell you the truth and you do not believe me?" He gave them an opportunity to find sin in Him and they could not! Their hypocrisy was exposed! Then they accused Him of being a Samaritan and proceeded in a last ditch effort to hurl their last insult—they accused Him of having a demon, but Jesus had the last word when He claimed to be 'I Am' (see John 8:48–59). This was too much for them, they were so enraged, they picked up stones to throw at Him but Jesus "hid Himself and went out of the temple, going through the midst of them, and so passed by (John 8:59). Their pride and hypocrisy was such that they were unwilling to accept the fact that the Messiah was standing in their midst and they were not willing to accept His God-given authority. We have to understand that Jesus obeyed the Law in every point—God's Law. It was only the traditions of men that Jesus did not obey. I think it is fair to say that Jesus abhorred the hypocritical attitudes of the experts who did not practice what they preached and who secretly sought to kill Him because His Word had no place in them (see John 8:38).

Another issue Jesus took to task was the attitude of the Pharisees who look down and even despise others. Jesus told the story of the Pharisee and the Tax Collector (see Luke 18:9–14) and how the Pharisee made a show of praying and boasting of his own moral and religious achievements. The tax collector however sensed his own unworthiness. Here are the words Jesus used Luke 18:14 "I tell you, this man went down to his house justified rather than the other; for everyone who exalts himself will be humbled, and he who humbles himself will be exalted." God is well able to exalt us when we are humble—we don't have to beg, we don't have to make life time vows to Him, we don't need a title, and we don't have to be 'a somebody,' but what we can do is trust Him. He has justified us, set us in the Kingdom of the Son of His love, He adopted us as His much-loved children, we belong to Him and all we have to do is trust Him. We do not have to perform, put up a front or boast of our achievements. Just trust! No more hypocrisy, the world can smell it a mile away and it stinks!

Chapter 19

GOD IS NOT ANGRY

John 3:17 says, "For God did not send His Son into the world to condemn the world, but that the world through Him might be saved." Jesus was talking to Nicodemus, a Pharisee who believed that the Messiah who was to come would be a judge as well as a Savior. For God so loved us, He gave us the choice that we might believe in Him and escape condemnation and punishment. How can God be angry when He has provided so great a salvation? He demonstrates His great love not His wrath towards us.

> "But God demonstrates His own love toward us, in that while we were still sinners, Christ died for us. Much more then, having now been justified by His blood, we shall be saved from wrath through Him." (Rom 5:8–9)

Psalm 103:8, 10–12 NKJV

> "The LORD is merciful and gracious, Slow to anger, and abounding in mercy… He has not dealt with us according to our sins, nor punished us according to our iniquities. For as the heavens are high above the

earth, So great is His mercy toward those who fear
Him; As far as the east is from the west, so far has
He removed our transgressions from us."

Clearly then God does not deal with us according to our sins, and just as well because none of us would make it. He deals with us according to the death of Jesus on the cross, His resurrection and ascension. I want you to know for sure that God is not angry with anyone—He is not handing out punishments and judging sin. How can I be so sure of this? Jesus calmed every life-threatening storm he encountered, He spoke to the wind and the waves. He never increased a calamity or suffering of any kind, He healed all who came to Him. Freedom and deliverance came to all, freely. When people encountered Jesus, it was just as if they had never sinned. He revealed the Father's heart of compassion for people who were to some extent terrorized by the religious system of the day. God is not angry with anyone. Yes, He hates injustice, hypocrisy etc.

Chapter 20

YOU CANNOT LOSE YOUR SALVATION

At another time, Jesus was in the temple at Solomon's porch on the Feast of Dedication, and the Jewish leaders surrounded Him wanting to know for sure if He really was the Messiah. Jesus replied—

John 10:25-39

> "I told you, and you do not believe. The works that I do in My Father's name, they bear witness of Me. But you do not believe, because you are not of My sheep, as I said to you. My sheep hear My voice, and I know them, and they follow Me. And I give them eternal life, and they shall never perish; neither shall anyone snatch them out of My hand. My Father, who has given them to Me, is greater than all; and no one is able to snatch them out of My Father's hand. I and My Father are one."

When Jesus said, "they shall never perish; neither shall anyone snatch them out of My hand and no one is able to snatch them out of His Father's hand," I am convinced that He meant it. Nothing has any power to snatch you out of His hand. Like the lost sheep, Jesus will go searching for you and carry you back on His shoulders to safety. Like the lost coin that never lost its value, God will search until He finds and rejoices over you. Like the prodigal son the Father's love makes everything right again. Jesus is the author and finisher of your faith (see Heb 12:2). You can be sure of this; He has all authority and power and He will complete what He began in you (see Php1:6), and your salvation is secure, nothing and no one can ever snatch you out of His hand.

We have a wonderful promise in John 5:24 that no matter what we have done or what we do in the future, we have the assurance of salvation. Jesus said, "Most assuredly, I say to you, he who hears My word and believes in Him who sent Me has everlasting life, and shall not come into judgment, but has passed from death into life."

Chapter 21

WHERE IS THE GOOD NEWS?

The good news in a nutshell is this—Jesus established a liberating, life-changing New Covenant (see Heb 8:13) based entirely on justification by faith (see Acts 13:38–39). Jesus did for us what legalism—law keeping, could not do for us. All the law can do now, is expose our sin, and tell us when we fail, it cannot cover, cleanse, make us righteous, holy or remove sins. Only the Blood of Jesus can do that, and it is all by grace through faith not by works. Now we have access to the throne room of God, grace, forgiveness and a loving God who will not condemn us. Now that has to be Good News! Right?

The Church is the primary vehicle through which the gospel of the Lord Jesus Christ is preached. If the church has lost the Truth for whatever reason, then where is the good news? Throughout church history, the good news of the Gospel of grace and no condemnation has come and gone. Have you ever thought why? Could it be because it brings freedom and the unmerited favor of God, and you can't control the people if they find out they are free, freely justified, forever forgiven and qualified to have a personal relationship with the One who created them. Fully qualified to read the bible for themselves with the guidance of the Promised Holy Spirit, free to get face to face with 'the book' and meditate on the truths in it. Free to make their own choices, run their own lives, free to fulfil their destiny, and free to be a disciple of Jesus. Freely given, freely received because it gives no place to pride and it is not selective.

Paul's letter to the Colossian church shows us how even believers in the first century church were at risk of being losing the Good News. His letter which was written about 60 AD strongly reminded believers not to listen to the false teachers who were spreading logic and man-made philosophies in an attempt to turn them away from the pre-eminence of the Lord Jesus Christ (see Col 1:18; 2:8). The Gnostics of the day thought they had the monopoly on the all knowledge and considered themselves experts who should be listened to. Paul warned believers not to be like them because their human logic led them away from the true knowledge of God. Paul prayed for the Colossian church that they might be pleasing to God, not pleasing to men, bearing fruits of righteousness, connected to Jesus, the vine, and most importantly personally increasing in the knowledge of God (see Col 1:9–10). Fear and pride will compel people to please men, instead of God. Human logic will always put the onus on the Christian to keep God's forgiveness by their own doing. There is no guilt or condemnation in the Good News. The Good News always liberates and exalts the finished work of Jesus on the cross. Increasing in the knowledge of how much God loves you will dissipate any fear and pride. This is Good News!

Paul encouraged the Ephesian church with these words—"But this is not the way of life that Christ has unfolded within you. If you have really experienced the Anointed One, and heard his truth, it will be seen in your life; for we know that the ultimate reality is embodied in Jesus!" (Eph 4:20–21 TPT).[24] You see, nothing happens in your life until you experience the Anointed

One then transformation comes. God will never use fear to scare you into submission or repentance; rather He woos you into intimate friendship with Him. Grace has a face, and His face is smiling, not condemning you. His love and mercy endures forever (see Psalm 118:1).

Chapter 22

CONTROL CANNOT BE IMPOSED

God's relationship with His people is based on relationship not control. God has freely given every one the fruit of self-control, so it has to come from within a believer not from leadership. Part of the church existing is to equip and empower people, thereby enabling them to discover the freedom that they have, which qualifies them to make their own good choices. It was for freedom that Christ set us free! The only acceptable control in church life therefore is self-control, which comes from the Holy Spirit (see Gal 5:22–23). The whole bible is about a living and relational God, who gave us a free-will, not about a God who demands submission, blind obedience and tedious law keeping. God produces sons and daughters who are co-workers with Him out of relationship which they freely choose. The Pharisees made their own rules; they knew more about their self-made structures, hierarchy, and systems of oppression than they knew of God. Thus they were inspired by a set of rules which had to be protected, not a relationship with God. The bible also tells us to submit to our leaders. True biblical submission is never imposed it is always voluntary and by free choice or it is worth nothing. [25]

Chapter 23

FAITH

Faith does not just believe there is a God; all that means is that you are not an atheist. Faith is more precious than gold (see 1 Peter 1:7), and that is why it is never a blind leap. Jesus said in Mark 11:22 "Have faith in God" so our faith has to be in God, and in what He has done. If we have faith in God for the abundant grace, which He promises to supply, we can face anything and it is sufficient for us to run the race marked out for us. Having faith in God to answer Paul's prayer for you and me "that we may walk worthy of the Lord, fully pleasing Him, being fruitful in every good work and increasing in the knowledge of God; strengthened with all might, according to His glorious power, for all patience and longsuffering with joy" (Col 1:10-11). Faith in God who strengthens us in Christ, so that we can speak to the mountains of anxiety, hopelessness, poverty, and oppression, etc. and see them move.

The bible also says that faith comes by hearing and hearing by the Word of God (see Rom 10:17). Thayer's definition for the word 'God' in the Greek is G5547 Χριστός, which is, translated Christos. 1) Christ was the Messiah, the Son of God. 2), anointed. Therefore, faith comes by hearing the Word of Christ, of grace, truth and no condemnation. The Passion Translation puts it like this "Faith, then is birthed in a heart that responds to God's anointed utterance of the Anointed One" (Romans 10:17). Faith comes, so you don't have to worry about having enough faith because Jesus is faithful and true, so we are safe in His care and that His grace keeps us faithful. Jesus is the author and finisher of a living faith that is why we look unto Him. Faith is born of the Holy Spirit in the hearts of people, because with the heart we believe.

God has a plan for us and we have to assume that He can do a better job of working it out than we can. The problem is that we want to be the producer, director and author of our destinies. The answer is not so much to let go and let God but rather to focus on Jesus and His ways and turn the pressure down by not searching for His will for you. 1 Thess 5:18 says, "He who calls you is faithful, who also will do it." So whatever His plan for you it will always be through the open door of grace.

Chapter 24

THERE IS NOTHING TO SEE HERE!

"Move along! There is nothing to see here!" (A catch phrase from the 1988 movie 'Naked Gun"). There is actually nothing to see except the Lord of Glory Himself in us, and the devil hates to see this because it reminds him of his humiliating defeat. Therefore, we have every right to say to the devil when he accuses us of past wrongdoing "Move along, there is nothing to see here!" There is no sin to see here! What about the sin we committed 5 minutes ago? There is still nothing to see because the Blood of Jesus is continually washing us clean. Look at 1 John 1:7 "But if we walk in the light as He is in the light, we have fellowship with one another, and the blood of Jesus Christ His Son cleanses us from all sin." Cleanses is a verb implying that the Blood of Jesus is continually cleansing us. The Passion Translation puts it this way "But if we keep living in the pure light that surrounds Him, we share unbroken fellowship with one another, and the blood of Jesus, his Son, continually cleanses us from all sin." Continually cleanses means that the cleansing does not stop, it has no end. The blood of Jesus keeps clean what it has already cleansed. Jesus saved us to the uttermost and He cleanses us from *all* sin. God has not only forgiven us, He cleans our conscience and the guilt that goes with it (see Heb 9:13–14) and it is not a once only event. No one else can do what Jesus can do for us, God is the only One who can go deep inside us and bring to light the deepest longing, the deepest hurt, pride, sin, and rejection. He deals with us on the fact that He is the God of mercy and grace. Can you see me jumping for joy?

Even though our sin is gone, I have to say that God still hates sin. God did not save us so we could keep on sinning and get away with it. Rather He gave us the ability to conquer sin by His grace. Rom 6:14 says, "For sin shall not have dominion over you, for you are not under law but under grace." Sin actually lost its dominion over you when we were born again. Therefore, while God does not remember or see our sin, His grace works in us to overcome sin.

Chapter 25

THERE IS NOTHING TO FEAR HERE!

Fear keeps too many of us from seeing the reality of His workmanship, if we think about it for a moment, God has gone to a lot of trouble to create many masterpieces by His skilled and thorough workmanship (see Eph 2:10) and then we go and compromise His work because of fear. Jesus did not fear the religious leaders of His day who openly opposed Him, He showed people how to live free and stay free of the confines of fear, religious law and the limitations it imposed. The Old Covenant of Law rejected the leper, a woman on her period and a dead body. God told Moses, in Numbers 5:2 "Command the children of Israel that they put out of the camp every leper, everyone who has a discharge and whoever becomes defiled by a corpse."[26] However, Jesus reached out and touched a leper (see Matt 8:1–4). He allowed a woman with a discharge to touch the hem of his garment (see Mark 5:25–34), and He held the hand of a dead girl and raised her back to life (see Mark 5:35–43). He gave the people a glimpse of the New Covenant He was about to bring in and demonstrated that there was no need to fear being contaminated by sinners, lepers or outcasts. He opened the eyes of a blind man (who wrongly thought to be cursed by God), and He was not afraid of those who opposed Him. He had already announced the acceptable year of the Lord, and he was not afraid to demonstrate it, even at the risk of scorn and contempt from the religious leaders. He healed everyone who came to Him. Luke 8:2 tells us that he healed certain women of evil spirits and infirmities—Mary called Magdalene, out of whom had come seven demons. He calmed storms which were wrongly thought to have been sent by God and He was not afraid of the blunders the disciples made, He was not afraid to give them power and authority over all demons and to cure diseases, and to send them out to preach the kingdom of God and heal the sick (see Luke 9:1-2). He was not afraid to allow women to be disciples along with the men (see Matt 27:55; Mark 15:41)[27]. He was not afraid to treat women equally, which went against the culture of the day. Not afraid to appoint seventy more disciples and give them authority to heal the sick and to say the kingdom of God has come near to you (see Luke 10:9). No fear here!

The portrayal of an angry God has caused many to be afraid of God. However, I cannot find any New Testament scripture that says God is full of wrath or angry with believers because of sin. God loved us while we were sinners and hostile toward Him, before we even knew anything about Him. We were never the object of His wrath—sin was. There really is nothing to be afraid of! There is nothing to fear here! If we wrongly think God is angry then we will not come to Him, we will shrink back and not get to the throne room to find grace to face life. In His presence, we change; He loves us better every time—He is the answer to every problem we can face.

God is holy and He has the heart of a Father as revealed by Jesus when He walked the earth. His love is perfect, He has already judged our sins and failings, mistakes and faults in the body of His Son Jesus. For God so loved us… Therefore, there is nothing to fear here, just love and mercy, because God goes before you, beside you, in fact, He is inside you and He will never leave you. God is faithful, He promised, and He will never abandon you.

Chapter 26

THERE IS NOTHING TO PAY HERE!

I often see this sign at the check in counters of airlines around the world, because the fare has been paid in full weeks beforehand. There is nothing to pay here because Jesus has already paid the redemption price in full on your behalf. God has freely given the gifts of abundant grace and righteousness that you might reign in life (see Rom 5:15,17).

God's anger against sin has been satisfied and today all we can expect from God is love, grace and truth not an invoice demanding payment. I cannot find any scriptures that say if we sin, we have to pay a penalty; or that God is counting your every sin, keeping a record of them in heaven, and weighing them up against the good things we have done. There is nothing to see or pay here! How is this good news? The word gospel means good news and the good news is that God is not counting your sins against you (see Psalm 103:8, Col 2:14), He cannot even if He wanted to because He has declared that He "will remember our sins no more." He has made a New Covenant—an entirely different one (see Heb 8:12–13, 10:17). Our debt for sin is 'paid in full!' The penalty cancelled. Is that good news or what?

Chapter 27

GOD IS NOT THE CHIEF OF THE FUN POLICE!

God is not the chief of the fun police, ready to arrest us and take us off to jail. Avoiding sin is not a test God sends us! The truth is we don't have to sin, because we are not slaves to sin anymore (see Rom 6:6) but we still have the choice. We can say "How about no thanks" to every temptation, we can resist and it will flee from us (see James 4:7). With God, there is no middle ground; it is slave to sin or slave to righteousness, there is no "no man's land."

There is no reason for us to be miserable—there is no reason why we cannot love God for what He has done. When we don't understand just how much we are loved we will try to exhibit more godliness and more good deeds and we give the impression that God is a hard task master, the chief of the fun police, and that He is only interested in what we Christians achieve. This is so far from the truth it is stupid!

Chapter 28

YOU DON'T *HAVE* TO BE PERFECT FOR GOD TO LOVE YOU!

God does not wait until we are perfect before He will love us because we will never be perfect and because He is perfect in all His ways. God looks at us and sees us as already perfect, that is why the Holy Spirit will only ever convict us of our righteousness. His love is blind! His love disciplines us, makes us holy and changes us. His love deals with our hypocrisy, double-mindedness, our insecurities and sin. It is by the power of His love that we can overcome every sin. God does not have to wait for us to clean ourselves up. Thank God for that!

We do not have to be perfect for God to love us—God is perfect love and he loves! God even loved us before we knew Him. His love matures us and makes us more like Him. The power of His love breaks the stoniest of hearts to pieces, and casts out our stupid fears. Our every weakness is overcome in His perfect, powerful loving presence and doing penance is not on God's program; we cannot do anything to make God love us!

1 John 4:1 says, "In this is love, not that we loved God, but that He loved us and sent His Son to be the propitiation for our sins." The word, "propitiation" means atonement, which in the English

thesaurus is "penance" so this is saying that Jesus did the penance, He made the amends, He took the punishment, He made the reparation, the recompense on our behalf. That leaves us with only one thing to do—accept it with humility! God does not even wait until we are perfect before He dwells within us. He waits for us to look to Him and acknowledge Him, He promised He would never leave us, He will love us all the way, and He will perfect us. There is only one way to the Father—through Jesus Christ, who is the way, the truth and the life! (see John 14:6).

Christians too often see themselves as unworthy or not good enough but God loves us all the same, He loved us when we were immature, rebellious and living the wild life! His perfect will for our lives is utterly astounding! When we grasp how wide and long and high and deep is the love of Christ and know that His love surpasses knowledge (see Eph 3:18), we will arise and shine for our light has come to us. We will be filled with fullness of God, and love and worship Him because He loved us first. His love makes us lovely! His love is unrelenting no matter what we are going through. What a King! What a Friend! What a God! Truly, there is none like Him!

Chapter 29

BODY BUILDING

We need strength for sure but it has to come from God not ourselves. Php 4:13 says, "I can do all things through Christ who strengthens me." What a huge promise, and such great strength can be matched with another great promise in James 1:5 "If any of you lacks wisdom, let him ask of God, who gives to all liberally and without reproach, and it will be given to him." With His strength, we really can do all the things that God has set for us. We can build spectacular, monumental monuments in our hearts to our magnificent, majestic God.

All of us at some time or other lack wisdom because the bible does not teach us how to handle life's problems but rather how to overcome them, instead of come under them. The bible does not say that we will live happily ever after (see John 16:33), but it does promise that when problems come there is wisdom, grace, strength and the power to see you through and come out the other end victorious. The bible does not teach us how to cope—it teaches us how to walk in victory. We do not have to rely on our wisdom but on God's infinite wisdom. That should make our hearts sing. So we ask for wisdom and faith, with no doubting (see James 1:6)—not up one minute and down the next, easy to say and hard to do, but the bible never says being a Christian is easy.

Chapter 30

"WHO DO YOU SAY I AM?"

The answer to the question what has God ever done for me can be found by asking another question that Jesus Himself asked, "Who do you say I Am?" When Jesus walked the earth, He was called many things! He was labelled and imposter (see John 8:48–59; 9:16; 10:20, Mark 2:6–7), and others though he was possessed by "Beelzebub, the ruler of the demons" (see Mark 3:21). Even his best friends thought, "He was out of His mind" (see Mark 3:21). Those who hated Him, purposefully attacked his integrity (see Matt 11:9), and sarcastically branded him as "a friend of sinners."

Who do you say that He is? A teacher, a radical man who verbally attacked religious leaders, a revolutionary, a moralist, a friend to the friendless? Many thought of Him as a hoax, but to every man, woman and child who encountered Him He was who He claimed to be—the Son of God, the Messiah.

When Jesus asked his disciples, "Who do you say I am?" Peter answered, "You are the Christ, the Son of the living God" (see Matt 16:15–16). This is who Jesus is; He is not only the Messiah but also God the Son.[28] The New Testament claims Jesus Christ is Lord (see Php 2:11). Paul wrote to the Colossians,

> "He (Jesus) is the image of the invisible God, the firstborn over all creation. For by Him all things were created that are in heaven and that are on earth, visible and invisible, whether thrones or dominions or principalities or powers. All things were created through Him and for Him. And He is before all things, and in Him all things consist. And He is the head of the body, the church, who is the beginning, the firstborn from the dead, that in all things He may have the pre-eminence. For it pleased the Father that in Him all the fullness should dwell, and by Him to reconcile all things to Himself, by Him, whether things on earth or things in heaven, having made peace through the blood of His cross" (Col 1:15–20).

John 1:1–3 declares, "In the beginning was the Word, and the Word was with God, and the Word was God. He was in the beginning with God. All things were made through Him, and without Him nothing was made that was made." John 1:14 says, "And the Word became flesh and dwelt among us, and we beheld His glory, the glory as of the only begotten of the Father, full of grace and truth." The Word who in the beginning was with God became a human. Why? Keeping it simple—Jesus said that he did not come not to destroy men's lives but to save them (Luke 9:56). He came to destroy the works of the devil (1 John 3:8) which he accomplished at Calvary (Col 2:15), He came to atone for our sins (1 John 2:2; 3:5), to give us eternal life (John 3:16) and He came that we might have abundant life (John 10:10). Most importantly, Jesus came to reveal to us not only the true nature of His Father God but our true nature as well.

Our true nature is in Him. In fact, our whole Christian life is lived in Him from start to eternity (1 Cor 1:2). We are the righteousness of God in Christ (2 Cor 5:21), made new creations in Him (2 Cor 5:17), brought near to God in Christ (Eph 2:13), and alive to God in Christ (Rom 6:11). We have the gift of no condemnation in Christ (Rom 8:1), set free from the bondage and curse of the law in Christ, and we are filled with the Holy Spirit in Christ. We are complete in Him (Col 2:9–10), we want to be found in Him not having our own righteousness which is from the law but through faith in Him (Php 3:9–10). We are hidden in Him (Col 3:3), in Him we live and move and have our being (Acts 17:28), in Him we are holy (1 Cor 1:2), and so much more.

Chapter 31

WHAT'S IN IT FOR YOU AND ME?

God saved us and called us with a holy calling according to His purpose (2 Timothy 1:9), we are chosen, predestined, adopted, accepted, redeemed, forgiven sealed with the Holy Spirit of Promise (Eph 1:13), and given an inheritance. Not only do we have a holy calling but also we have a high calling (Phil 3:4) and a heavenly calling (Hebrew 3:1). This is for you and me, and this is how it is supposed to be. We get to have the pleasure of co-partnering with the Lord Jesus Christ in His great plan of salvation for the world and that is why Jesus Himself raised us up and made us sit together in the heavenly places in Him and all because of His great love (Eph 2:4–6).

Who am I, and what am I doing here? The answer to this age-old question is found in the life, death and resurrection of Jesus Christ. Your life has meaning in the One who created it.[29] Jesus had a plan and it would take more than twelve men, it takes you and me and it is to our advantage. It takes walking by faith not by sight, and it takes Holy Spirit power and great grace in you and me (see Acts 4:33). On the cross, Jesus declared, "It is finished!" Jesus has overcome the world, the ultimate sacrifice has been made—now it is up to those who are freely justified by His grace to embrace it and do what He did.

Chapter 32

THE TRUTH IS DANGEROUS

When Jesus said that the world would hate them have you ever thought about why that would be so? The truth is dangerous, it sets free when known, and it stirs up religious spirits even to the point of murder. The Pharisees, who were experts in the law, actually broke the law by planning a murder, and they did not even recognize the author of the law when He was standing in front of them. It is interesting that the ones society ignored knew who Jesus was and acknowledged Him but not the educated leaders who had all the knowledge of the Law.

The danger to the Galatian Church in the first Century was not persecution from outside but false teaching from the inside. The gospel of grace as well Paul's apostolic ministry was under attack by those who wanted to mix grace with the keeping of the law. Paul preached the truth of the Gospel of grace and his preaching stirred up hatred towards him. At Lystra he was stoned by a multitude who dragged him out of the city, supposing him to be dead (see Acts 14:19). Stephen and James the brother of John, (see Acts 12:2) were martyred. Jesus actually told Peter that he would be martyred, in fact Peter had already said that he would lay down his life for the Lord (see John 21:19–21) and John was an exile on the Island of Patmos.

Opposition is inevitable! In first century Jerusalem after Pentecost, the streets were crowded with Christians and the Judaizers[30] were alarmed. The moment they heard the guard's report of the empty tomb, they bribed them with a large sum of money to spread the lie that the disciples of Jesus came and stole the body at night, and if the governor heard about it they would appease him so that the guards would not be executed (see Matt 28:11–14). Opposition came with intensity! The disciples were warned to stop teaching in the Name of Jesus (see Acts 4:5–18), they were thrown into prison, and when the prison could not hold them they were threatened with death and would have been killed on the spot (see Acts 5:33) had not a Pharisee named Gamaliel intervened (see Acts 5:34–39). However, they went on preaching as if nothing had happened, nothing could stop the fire of the Holy Spirit burning in the hearts of ordinary people who had an encounter with the risen Lord. The Persecution began with the death of Stephen (see Acts 7:59) and the message of the Good News spread rapidly to the rest of the known world.

Jesus talked to His closest friends in the Upper Room about how to live the Christian life, He talked about His love for them and the provisions He made for them. He never said it would be easy— in fact, He made it clear that the world would hate them. "The early Christians were the targets of repeated persecutions—some of unspeakable cruelty. For example, the emperor Nero blamed the Christians for the great fire that destroyed ten of the fourteen city wards at Rome in 64 A.D., a fire that Nero apparently had ordered himself. The historian Tacitus, not a Christian, said that Nero had the believers "torn by dogs, nailed to crosses . . . even used as human torches to illumine his gardens at night."[31]

Herod about 44 A.D (Acts 12:2) executed James the son of Zebedee. Early Latin tradition has John escaping unhurt after being cast into boiling oil at Rome. Researcher David Barrett reports that by the year 300, or nine generations after Christ, the world was 10.4% Christian with 66.4% of believers Non-whites. The scriptures had been translated into ten languages. More than 410,000, representing one in every 200 believers from the time of Christ, had given their lives as martyrs for the faith.[32]

After Jesus told the twelve that the world would hate them He washed their feet and took the position of a slave, giving them an example of what their future was to hold when He was not physically present (see John 13:1). Jesus forewarned them that He would be leaving them, John 16:7 says, "Nevertheless I tell you the truth. It is to your advantage that I go away; for if I do not go away, the Helper will not come to you; but if I depart, I will send Him to you." His purpose in coming was to die (see Mark 10:45) so He could finish the work He was sent to do, and so He could send the Holy Spirit to be with them, guide them into all truth, show them things to come, glorify Jesus and reveal things to them (see John 16:13–15). We are never alone!

Chapter 33

AGREEING WITH GOD

God wants us to be constantly thinking that we are forever forgiven, lavishly loved, made remarkably righteous, that we are permanently, perpetually, stupendously and spectacularly saved, and it is all unconditionally and overwhelmingly free—paid in full because that is the truth. Why? Because God wants us to think the same way about ourselves as He does. Col 1:22 says, "He has reconciled in the body of His flesh through death, to present you holy, and blameless, and above reproach *in His sight.*" God sees us as holy, blameless and restored, above accusation and criticism. In God's sight, you are precious, priceless and prized as a holy priesthood (see 1 Peter 2:4). We really should agree with God here! God will never count your sin against you! We are under the New Covenant that Jesus came to declare— "the acceptable year of the Lord" (see Luke 4:19). The time of God's unconditional acceptance of you and me.

We live lives that are true to the Holy Spirit who lives *in* us. The Holy Spirit is holy in every way you can think of. Holiness by the way is not being in the state of sinlessness—rather holiness is being in the world but not of it. Holiness means set apart unto God, which occurred when you were born again. Holiness is a life of allowing God to change you. True holiness does not come from striving it flows from a heart set free from condemnation. Want to be holy? Stop striving to be holy and allow God's love to woo you. Jesus loves you into holiness because He is holy. The secret to godliness, character and holiness is in Him, when we are in Him—we are godly, righteous and holy.

Chapter 34

REIGNING IN LIFE

We are disciples, and we are to be like the Master, so it is vital that we see ourselves and others the way God sees us. It is important then to take responsibility for our personal walk with God and study the scripture for ourselves. There may be times when we feel helpless, God seems silent, and no amount of praying brings answers. These moments can test us severely, but they can also bring forth the fruit in our lives that will remain. This is when we get to do something! At last, we pick up our weapons and fight the good fight of faith. When the going gets tough the tough get going. This is when we get to do something at last.

Romans 5:17

> "For if by the one man's offense death reigned through the one, much more those who receive abundance of grace and of the gift of righteousness will reign in life through the One, Jesus Christ."

Reigning in life does not mean ruling over people, because God created us with a free will, it means you rule over yourself and that makes you responsible, so when contrary things happen, you get to decide if you should give it significance or not. It means you rule over the wrong opinions of the culture you live in. In other words, those devastating circumstances don't rule over you and pull you down. We have the "keys to the Kingdom" (see Matt 16:19) which is the authority to trample all over the powers of darkness (see Luke 10:19), we have access to the abundance of grace and the gift of righteousness so we reign in life through the One—Jesus Christ. We have influence over the strategies of darkness, as well our own free will.

So how do you reign in life? When David as a boy faced the giant Goliath, he was armed with knowledge and a good memory, as well as five smooth stones. He knew some very important things that helped him face a man of whom everyone was afraid. He knew who God was, he knew who he was and he knew about his enemy. If we know God and know who we are (in God) and know the wiles of the devil then the devil cannot deceive us, or taunt us like Goliath did to the Israelites (see 1 Samuel 17). We have to not only know who we are but remember it as well, so we can use the Shield of Faith and the Sword of the Spirit against the enemy and experience the victory that is already ours. Just as Jesus did when tempted by the devil in the desert. Jesus used the Word of God as a weapon to silence the enemy. However, just memorizing scripture will not enlighten us it has to be a "lamp to our feet and a light to our path" (see Psalm 119:105). It is important to remember that sometimes temptation comes (see Matt 4:1), and sometimes the most powerful enemy is ourselves so we have to do some serious self-talking and mix the Word of God with Holy Spirit and grace and use it on ourselves.

Study the Word of God for yourself; ask the question "Does this make sense to the people to whom it was written?" The text must make sense to its original hearers; this involves finding answers to who, what, where, when, why and how. Jesus said to the lawyers in Luke 11:52, "Woe to you lawyers! For you have taken away the key of knowledge. You did not enter in yourselves, and those who were entering in you hindered." People looked to the lawyers for the interpretation of the truth, they were experts in the law, and so they interpreted God's truth with a legalistic approach and this did not help the people at all, in fact it was a hindrance. Jesus accused them of taking away the key of knowledge—they did this by substituting the truth with the Law and their traditions, which were all about performance and not about what God had done for them. Do not get me wrong here the law is holy, and the commandments holy, just and good, (Romans 7:12) but they cannot make you holy, just or good. All the law can do is inform you that you are definitely not holy, nor just nor good. Therefore, the good news is—we have a Savior who is good on our behalf. God blesses us not because we are good but because He is good.

It is the abundance of grace and the gift of righteousness that causes us to reign in life, not our achieving or our impressing others or the culture, or the country we live in, or how much money we have or do not have. It is through nothing that we can ever do except to accept and believe that Jesus has done it all for us. We cannot achieve salvation, grace, or righteousness because they are gifts so all we can do is receive it and say thank you Lord. Once received then we have to unwrap it and use it—a gift is not a gift if you have to work for it, it becomes a wage. No one alive deserves this gift and Jesus did not deserve to pay the wages for our sin either. The bible says in 2 Corinthians 5:21 "For He made Him who knew no sin to be sin for us, that we might become the righteousness of God in Him." So the least we can do is accept that He paid our debt in full, and by His death, he achieved grace and righteousness for us, so now we do not have to achieve anything, but simply receive the gift.

Chapter 35

WONDERS IN THE WORD

What has God done for you? God has done exactly what the law or you and I could never do! God has wiped out the power and record of sin in our lives. God has not put the record on the shelf or kept it in a vault until judgment day. It has been crucified with Jesus on the cross of Calvary—Jesus took it to hell and left it there and rose from the dead triumphant! It is finished! Now we are free to live the resurrected life in the Lord Jesus. One of the greatest things God ever created is our free will, because we now get to become lovers of God and willing co-laborers with Him. I hope you know by now that once you accepted salvation, the Blood of Jesus wiped out your sin forever, so we cannot get any cleaner. The great apostle Paul even addressed believers as saints, Jesus called us friends and God calls us sons and daughters. The point is we have a privileged relationship with an Almighty Loving God whose love transforms us. The whole gospel is a story of God wooing the hearts of humanity through His love. This requires a response from us based solely on the operation of our free will.

What exactly has God done? He has done exactly what you and I could never do.

God has transferred His righteousness to you and declared that you are justified by faith alone. Now you have peace with God (Rom 5:1).

God has rescued you from the powers of darkness and put you in the Kingdom of His Son (Col 1:13).

He has cancelled the debt you owe for your sins and made Jesus pay for it (Col 1:14).

He has forever forgiven you all your sins (Col 2:13).

God has removed your sin from you as far as the east is from the west (Psalm 103:12).

God has totally set you free from every trace of sin by the power of the Blood of Jesus (1 John 1:7).

He has cut away (circumcised) all the guilt and the power of sin and removed it all from you (Col 2:11).

God has totally wiped out your record of wrongdoing. He cancelled it, and it cannot be dragged up again ever because He totally erased it by nailing on the cross of Jesus, and not only that made a public display of the cancellation (Col 2:14).

God has closed the case, found you not guilty; no one can condemn you now because He has placed you in Christ Jesus (Rom 8:1).

God has redeemed you from the curse of the Law, by Jesus being made a curse for you, so that Abraham's blessing can come to you that you might receive the promise of the Holy Spirit through faith (Gal 3:13-14).

God has given you perfect standing with Him. He has washed you of every weakness, sanctified you and all because of the Name of the Lord Jesus and the Spirit of God (1 Cor 6:11).

God has made you a brand new person, He recreated you in righteousness and true holiness (Eph 4:24).

God has paid the price for you to be without guilt, Jesus took the punishment that makes you whole (Isa 53:5).

God has cleansed you, made you holy and acquitted you in the Name of the Lord Jesus and by the Spirit of God (1 Cor 6:11).

God sent Jesus to die for you because of His great love (John 3:16)

God has forgiven you <u>all</u> your sins (Col 1:14, 2:13; Eph 1:7; Titus 2:14; Rom 4:6–8; 1 John 1:9).

God has made Jesus who knew no sin to be sin for you (2 Cor 5:21).

God has reconciled to Himself through Jesus Christ and given you the ministry of reconciliation (2 Cor 5:18).

God has put all your shame, all your weaknesses and sicknesses on Jesus and Jesus took it on Himself on the cross; all for you (Isa 53:10; Matt 8:17).

God has crucified you in Christ, He has made you free from sin and given you fruit to holiness and everlasting life (Rom 6:22-23).

God has accepted you in the beloved, he has redeemed you through the Blood of Jesus; you have the forgiveness of sins and all according to the riches of His grace (Eph 1:6–7).

God has made your heart pure now you can follow the ways of righteousness, faith, love and peace (2 Tim 2:22).

He has called you according to His purposes (Rom 8:27–30).

God has made His grace abundantly available for you and it is enough for you (2 Cor 12:9).

God has made you a chosen generation, a royal priesthood, a holy nation, a person set apart He has called me out of darkness into His marvelous light (1 Peter 2:9).

God has given you a new heart and put a new spirit in you. He has taken your heart of stone and replaced with a new heart. He put His very own Spirit in you and He causes you to walk in His statutes. (Psalm 51:10; Eze 36:26–27).

God has made you more than a conqueror through Him (Rom 8:37), and He has given you the victory through Jesus Christ (1 Cor 15:57).

God has given you a victorious life, the resurrection life, and a fresh new start—a new life (Col 3:1–3).

God has established you in righteousness and true holiness (Eph 4:24).

God has given you the oil of joy for mourning, and the garment of praise for depression. He calls you a tree of righteousness. You are the planting of the Lord, that He might be glorified (Isa 61:3).

God has given you the power to hold yourself calm in the days of adversity (Psalm 94:13).

God has placed you in His kingdom of righteousness, peace and joy in the Holy Spirit (Rom 14:17).

God has brought you out of the miry clay and set your feet upon a rock (Psa 40:2–3).

God has given you a measure of faith (Rom 12:3).

God has borne your grief and carried your sorrow (Isa 53:4)

God has predestined your life according to His plan (Eph 1:11).

God fearfully and wonderfully created you (Psalm 139:14).

God has strengthened you with all power according to His glorious might (Col 1:11–12).

God has given you peace like a river and righteousness and forgiveness like the waves of the sea (Isa 48:18). His peace surpasses all understanding, guards you heart and mind through Christ Jesus. (Php 4:6–7).

God has given you the sure hope of your salvation (1 Thess 5:8).

God has made Jesus your Head, the Head of the church and the Head of all principality and power (Col 2:10; Eph 1:22)

God made Jesus to be poor for your sake so that you might be made rich (2 Cor 8:9).

God has made His wisdom which is pure, then peaceable, gentle, full of mercy, good fruits, without partiality and without hypocrisy available to you (James 3:17).

God has supplied you with mighty weapons to pull down the stronghold of fear (2 Cor 10:4).

God has given you the spirit of wisdom and understanding, the spirit of counsel and might, the spirit of knowledge and of the fear of the Lord (Isa 11:1–3).

God has given you faith, which does not stand in the wisdom of men, but in the power of God (1 Cor 2:5).

God has chosen you to an inheritance, He has predestined you according to His purpose and He works all things out for your good (Eph 1:11, Rom 8:28). How good is that?

God has made you His workmanship and created you to do good works according to His righteousness and holiness (Eph 2:10, 2:23–24).

God has rescued you from a dead end life. He has set you into the Kingdom of the Son He loves (Col 1:13).

God has redeemed you from the curse of poverty and made Abraham's blessing available to you by faith. He has made you Abraham's seed and an heir (Gal 3:13, 14, 16, 29).

God has made all grace abound toward you for every good work (2 Cor 9:8).

God has made a covenant with you and your descendants after you (Gen 9:9).

God has made you alive to God through Jesus Christ your Lord (Rom 6:11).

God has clearly made known to you His creation, eternal power and Godhead so you are without excuse (Rom 1:19–20).

God has given you the promise of rest from working for your salvation (Heb 4:1, 9), and that He will give you rest (Matt 11:28).

God has given you great everlasting joy and blessing and He adds no sorrow with it (Prov 10:22).

God has put His Word near you, in your mouth and in your heart, that if you confess with your mouth the Lord Jesus and believe in your heart that God raised Him from the dead, you will be saved (Rom 10:8–9).

God has blessed you with every spiritual blessing in Christ (Eph 1:3).

God has made know to you the mystery of His will (Eph 1:9).

God has made the exceeding greatness power toward you who believe which He worked in in Christ when He raised Jesus from the dead and seated Him at His right hand (Eph 1:19).

God made you alive when you were dead in sin and made His mercy available because of His great love and He raised you up to sit in heavenly places in His Son (Eph 2:1–6).

God has prepared good works for you to do (Eph 2:10).

God has brought you near to Him by the Blood of Jesus (Eph 2:13).

God has made Jesus your Head and given Him first place in your life (Col 1:19).

God has put Jesus in you and you in Jesus

God has put you in Christ and made you an entirely new creation with all things made new (2 Cor 5:17).

God has put the living Christ in you, the hope of Glory (Col 1:27).

He has now hidden your life in His Son Jesus, now when He looks at you He sees Jesus (Col 3:3).

God has clothed you with the Lord Jesus Christ (Rom 13:13).

God has put His Holy Spirit in you, and He makes your body alive (Rom 8:11) and He has given you the victory over death through Jesus Christ (1 Cor 15:57).

God has implanted His Word in you (James 1:21).

God has clothed you with the Lord Jesus Christ (Rom 13:13).

God has raised you up and made you sit together in heavenly places in Christ Jesus (Eph 2:6).

God has made your way perfect (2 Sam 22:33), He has put you in Christ Jesus and given you grace, wisdom, righteousness, sanctification and redemption (1 Cor 1:30, Eph 1:7).

God has chosen you in Him before the foundation of the world (Eph 1:4).

God has made you complete in Jesus who is the Head of every kingdom and authority, He has filled you with Himself (Col 2:10).

God has made you perfect, holy and complete for all time (Heb 10:13).

God has made it possible for you to enter His presence

God has made it possible for you to boldly enter into the Holy of Holies, without hesitation, by the Blood of Jesus (Heb 10:19).

God raised you up and seated you with Christ in heavenly places, and just because of His great love (Eph 2:6).

God has always loved you

God loves you with a great love that even when you are living a life of sin, the bible calls it *dead* in sin God made you *alive* in Christ (Eph 2:5).

God so loves you that He sent Jesus to die for you, so that everyone who believes in Him will not perish but have everlasting life (John 3:16).

God has promised you that nothing shall be able to separate you from His love, which is in Jesus (Rom 8:39).

God has poured out His love upon you, and given you true hope that does not disappoint (Romans 5:5). A confident hope that only expects the good in every situation.

God has set His love on you; He has made a safe place for you to take shelter and refuge under His wings (Psalm 91).

God has made you in His image, He has made you His elect, holy and beloved (Col 3:10–12).

God has honored you in His sight; He has not ever rejected you (Isa 43:4). God has called you, by your name; you are His (Isa 43:1).

God formed you and created you for His glory (Isa 43:7).

God has strengthened you with power of the Holy Spirit

God has strengthened you with power through the Holy Spirit who lives in you (Eph 3:16).

God makes your body alive through the Holy Spirit who dwells in you (Rom 8:11), and gives you the victory over death through Jesus Christ (1 Cor 15:57).

God has given you righteousness peace and joy in the Holy Spirit (Rom 14:17).

He has sealed you with the Holy Spirit of promise (Eph 1:13).

God has filled you full of the Holy Spirt and where the Spirit of the Lord is, there is liberty (2 Cor 3:17).

God has baptized you with the Holy Spirit and freely given you the gifts of the Holy Spirit (1 Cor 12:4, 30; Rom 11:29).

He sent the Holy Spirit to help you, to comfort you and He will never leave you (John 14:6).

He has given you a spirit of power and of love and of a sound mind (2 Tim 1:7).

God has made you a son or daughter of His

God has adopted you into His family. You are His child, He sent the Spirit of His Son into your heart so you can call Father God your Father (Gal 4:6).

Through faith in Jesus, God has made you a son or daughter of His (Gal 3:26).

He has given you a Spirit of Adoption (Rom 8:15), and an heir of His through Jesus Christ (Gal 4:7).

God created you, formed you and redeemed you. He called you by your name, now you belong to Him (Isa 43:1).

God as predestined you to be adopted a son or daughter by Jesus Christ according to the pleasure of His good will (Eph 1:5).

God has taken ownership of you now you belong to Him as a chosen generation, a royal priesthood, a holy nation, a person set apart to speak His praises. He has you called out of darkness into His marvelous light (1 Peter 2:9).

God has made Jesus the Author and Finisher of your faith so you can always look to Him (Heb 12:2).

It is a fact – God has officially adopted you, you are under His love and protection and covering, His love covers everything. You belong to God!

Romans 8:15

> For you did not receive the spirit of bondage again
> to fear, but you received the Spirit of adoption by
> whom we cry out, "Abba, Father."

Galatians 3:26

> For you are all sons of God through faith in Christ
> Jesus.

All sons have full rights there are no exceptions! To whom was Paul speaking? In this chapter Paul writes using the word "we", but in verse 26 he uses the word "you" and does so for the rest of the chapter (which is only three more verses). Who is "the you?" Verse 27 tells us—He was talking about all the ones baptized into Christ That is you and I!

Galatians 4:7

> "Therefore you are no longer a slave but a son, and
> if a son, then an heir of God through Christ."

Every born again person, male or female, boy or girl in the bible is a *"son"*. We are all sons of God through Jesus. We are all one in Christ (Verse 28). I cannot find any expression in the New Testament, which calls me a daughter of God, with the exception of 2 Cor 6:18, which is a quote from the Old Testament. 1 John 3:2 says, "Beloved, now we are children of God; and it has not yet been revealed what we shall be, but we know that when He is revealed, we shall be like Him, for we shall see Him as He is." We shall all be like Him.

Galatians 3:27-28

> For as many of you as were baptized into Christ have
> put on Christ. There is neither Jew nor Greek, there
> is neither slave nor free, there is neither male nor
> female; for you are all one in Christ Jesus.

Our standing before God is in Jesus. God looks at you and me
and sees Jesus and that makes us one in Him. You belong to God!
This then would have to be *in my opinion* the most profound thing
that I can get out of the Word of God. You and I belong to God;
He has taken ownership of us, adopted us into His family and
it is forever. He will never leave us, nor forsake us! We are the
forgiven, and this says to me that we cannot lose our salvation.
God will never abandon us—He cannot, because we are His sons
and daughters.

Romans 8:17

> "and if children, then heirs—heirs of God and joint
> heirs with Christ, if indeed we suffer with Him,
> that we may also be glorified together."

Not only are we sons of God but also heirs of God. Jesus went to
the cross to get his inheritance. Does that mean we have to too?
Yes, we die to ourselves we put to death our selfish old nature
and put on the resurrected us. However, concentrate on the part
of the scripture that declares we are heirs of God and joint heirs
with Christ.

Ephesians 1:13

> In Him you also trusted, after you heard the word
> of truth, the gospel of your salvation; in whom also,

having believed, you were sealed with the Holy
Spirit of promise,

The Holy Spirit sealed the deal with Himself guaranteeing your
salvation. You are stamped with God's approval! Do not let anyone
tell you otherwise especially yourself!

1 Corinthians 3:16

Do you not know that you are the temple of God
and that the Spirit of God dwells in you?

Here is some trivia for you; Paul asked this question thirteen times
in various epistles; I think he wanted you to remember who you
are. You are a carrier of God and God is ever-present in you!

2 Corinthians 5:17

Therefore, if anyone is in Christ, he is a new
creation; old things have passed away; behold, all
things have become new.

Let us get this settled if God is in you your old life is gone. It is
only a memory, it has passed away, gone dead and buried. You
have received a new life to take its place and now you have a new
and living adventure every day to encounter, a radical life to live.
Go get it!

Ephesians 2:10

For we are His workmanship, created in Christ Jesus
for good works, which God prepared beforehand
that we should walk in them.

In this new and living way there are good God works for you to do; works which God has already worked out for you to work out. Remember these amazing works do not save us and yet somehow it all works out for your good.

Ephesians 4:24

> And that you put on the new man which was created according to God, in true righteousness and holiness.

This new you was created in righteousness and true holiness; righteousness means made after the image of God and holiness is not pretend holiness but true cleanness of heart and mind and you can put it on.

Psalms 91:1–11

> He who dwells in the secret place of the Most High Shall abide under the shadow of the Almighty. I will say of the LORD, "He is my refuge and my fortress; My God, in Him I will trust." Surely He shall deliver you from the snare of the fowler and from the perilous pestilence. He shall cover you with His feathers, and under His wings you shall take refuge; His truth shall be your shield and buckler. You shall not be afraid of the terror by night, nor of the arrow that flies by day, Nor of the pestilence that walks in darkness, nor of the destruction that lays waste at noonday. A thousand may fall at your side, and ten thousand at your right hand; but it shall not come near you. Only with your eyes shall you look, and see the reward of the wicked. Because you have made the LORD, who is my refuge, Even the Most

High, your dwelling place, No evil shall befall you, nor shall any plague come near your dwelling; For He shall give His angels charge over you, to keep you in all your ways.

Do you get this? This says that God covers you with His feathers and under His wings, there is refuge, and His truth is your shield and buckler. (Verse 4, 5). A 'buckler' in Hebrew is sôchêrâh—*something surrounding the person, that is, a shield—buckler.* You have protection all the time! You are safe! You are a precious child of the Almighty God, who actually lives in you!

Romans 12:11

"Not lagging in diligence, fervent in spirit, serving the Lord;"

Being *"fervent in spirit"* means to boil. The Greek word is 'zeo' it means to boil with heat. We have a responsibility to stay hot no matter what! How? Get into the Word of God. Your zeal will ignite, when you hear God speak to you through the pages of the bible. I am not talking about a religiously reading the bible, I am talking about desperately digging into the Scriptures to find truth. The disciples on the Emmaus Road said, "Were not our hearts burning within us while He was explaining the scriptures to us." (Luke 24:32). Their hearts were *'zeo'* boiling with heat, and set ablaze! You know God invested a lot of time and energy to give us His Word, and many people gave their lives so that we could have a copy. It is His love letter to you!

Maybe you have not had time for God to speak to you in His Word, or maybe you have pain or failure, it doesn't matter to God He is available at any time. You can begin afresh right now. Just approach God; when Jesus approached His Father in anguish He began with "O My Father... In the Garden of Gethsemane Jesus went to the Throne Room to find grace to help in His time of need. He found grace to face the trial. Embrace grace and you can run the race. You have grace available to face any race. Go for it! Then praise God with abandon, and watch new strength arise in you

EPILOGUE

Christianity is where the believer is, this is where the rubber meets the road. Christians are a called out people, called out of the world's system of a manmade culture, legalism, power plays and manipulation. The called out ones are called to be worshipers, not just in church, because He is worthy of our praise. It is not about where you worship—it is about how you worship Him that is important. Jesus said that worshipers will worship the Father in spirt and truth (John 4:23). True worship can be anywhere, and at any time. As with all things in God, it is by faith and by the Spirit of God that we give praise and worship to God. When church structure is more important than the individual is, then people with a heart for God, the called out ones, will leave the structure in order to pursue a relationship with Him that enables them to dream, and be fulfilled because God Himself has put that desire in them. When people encounter God this way they will grow, they will move further and further into the hands of a relational, intimate and loving Father God. Jeremiah 29:11 says "For I know the thoughts that I think toward you, says the LORD, thoughts of peace and not of evil, to give you a future and a hope."

It is not only God's desire for everyone to be saved but to also come the intimate knowledge of the truth—the Lord Jesus—for themselves (see 1 Timothy 2:4). Michael and Arthur needed to know the truth in their hearts that they were on the Father's heart and mind from the start and that His unending love is great towards them. They needed to get face to face with a book called the bible, face to face with the Holy Spirit and what God has really done for them will come alive.

You are who God says you are! It is only when we see ourselves the way God created us to be that we can really know who we are and who God is. Jesus said in John 15:1 "You did not choose Me, but I chose you and appointed you that you should go and bear fruit, and that your fruit should remain, that whatever you ask the Father in My name He may give you." We are not our own, God has chosen us not because we are special but because His goodness has chosen and ordained us. This truth alone, the Lord Jesus Himself makes us someone very special. Knowing that God has chosen you and appointed you to bear fruit—no matter who you are—is a life changing truth because now we can ask the Father In Jesus Name that He may give it to us.

God has done all this and none of it was because of anything you have done or have not done—Jesus accomplished it all. Why would God do all this for you? Because of His great love!

ENDNOTES

Chapter 2

[1] "Luke and Acts: To the Lovers of God", © 2014 The Passion Translation. Translated directly from the original Greek and Aramaic texts by Dr. Brian Simmons Published by BroadStreet Publishing Group, LLC Racine, Wisconsin USA

Chapter 4

[2] The World's Greatest Revivals © 2007- Fred and Sharon Wright DESTINY IMAGE PUBLISHERS PO Box 310, Shippensburg, PA 17257-0310

[3] The World's Greatest Revivals © 2007- Fred and Sharon Wright DESTINY IMAGE PUBLISHERS PO Box 310, Shippensburg, PA 17257-0310

[4] Ten Lies the Church Tells Women by Lee J Grady published by Charisma House, Charisma Media/Charisma House Book Group 600 Rinehart Road, Lake Mary, Florida 32746)

[5] Ten Lies the Church Tells Women by Lee J Grady published by Charisma House, Charisma Media/Charisma House Book Group 600 Rinehart Road, Lake Mary, Florida 32746)

6   Ten Lies The Church Tells Women by Lee J Grady published by Charisma House, Charisma Media/Charisma House Book Group 600 Rinehart Road, Lake Mary, Florida 32746.

7   Ten Lies The Church Tells Women by Lee J Grady published by Charisma House, Charisma Media/Charisma House Book Group 600 Rinehart Road, Lake Mary, Florida 32746.

8   © 2014 The Passion Translation Letters from Heaven by the Apostle Paul, Translated directly from the original Greek and Aramaic texts by Dr Brian Simmons. Published by BroadStreet Publishing Group, LLC Racine, Wisconsin USA

9   © 2014 The Passion Translation Letters from Heaven by the Apostle Paul, Translated directly from the original Greek and Aramaic texts by Dr. Brian Simmons. Published by BroadStreet Publishing Group, LLC Racine, Wisconsin USA

Chapter 5

10   Destined to Reign" by Joseph Prince ©Joseph Prince, 2011 Joseph Prince Teaching Resources www.josephprinceonline.com

Chapter 6

11   "The World's Greatest Revivals" authors Fred and Sharon Wright (© 2007 Fred and Sharon Wright, Destiny Image Publishers, INC PO Box 310, Shippington, PA 17257-0310

Chapter 8

12   Simmons, Brian. The Passion Translation New Testament (2nd Edition): With Psalms, Proverbs and Song of Songs. BroadStreet Publishing Group LLC. Kindle Edition.

13   Simmons, Brian. The Passion Translation New Testament (2nd Edition): With Psalms, Proverbs and Song of Songs. BroadStreet Publishing Group LLC. Kindle Edition.

Chapter 9

14   The Seven Principles for Making Marriage Work, © 1999 John Gottman, Ph. D, and Nan Silver, Published by Three Rivers Press, New York, New York. Random House, Inc. New York, Toronto, London, Sydney, Auckland. www.randomhouse.com Chapter 6, Principle 4.

15   10 Lies the Church Tells women by J Lee Grady. © 2000, 2006 by J Lee Grady Published by Charisma House, Charisma Media/ Charisma House Book Group 600 Rinehart Road Lake Mary, Florida 32746 www.charismahouse.com

16   The word used in this passage manage G3616 means to be the head of the house. They were to rule their homes. (G3616 οἰκοδεσποτέω oikodespoteō Thayer Definition: 1) to be master (or head) of a house 2) to rule a household, manage family affairs Part of Speech: verb A Related Word by Thayer's/Strong's Number: from G3617 Citing in TDNT: 2:49, 145

17   The Seven Principles for Making Marriage Work, © 1999 John Gottman, Ph. D, and Nan Silver, Published by Three Rivers Press, New York, New York. Random House, Inc. New York, Toronto, London, Sydney, Auckland. www.randomhouse.com Chapter 6, Principle 4, Page 100.

18   The Seven Principles for Making Marriage Work, © 1999 John Gottman, Ph. D, and Nan Silver, Published by Three Rivers Press, New York, New York. Random House, Inc. New York, Toronto, London, Sydney, Auckland. www.randomhouse.com Chapter 6, Principle 4, Page 102.

19   https://en.wikipedia.org/wiki/Wives_of_King_Henry_VIII

20   Simmons, Brian. The Passion Translation New Testament (2nd Edition): With Psalms, Proverbs and Song of Songs. BroadStreet Publishing Group LLC. Kindle Edition.

Chapter 12

21   Read more at: https://www.brainyquote.com/quotes/james_a_garfield_140609

Chapter 16

22   https://edition.cnn.com/2017/09/14/politics/kfile-roy-moore-9-11/index.html Article by Andrew Kaczynski and Nathan McDermott, CNN Updated 2048 GMT (0448 HKT) 4 September 14, 2017

23   https://www.abc.net.au/news/2019-11-18/sydney-morning-briefing-monday-november-18/11712170

Chapter 21

24   Simmons, Brian. The Passion Translation New Testament (2nd Edition): With Psalms, Proverbs and Song of Songs. BroadStreet Publishing Group LLC. Kindle Edition.

Chapter 23

25   "The Greek word for submission is hupotasso it is written in the middle voice, which means it is something that an individual imposes upon himself or herself. It means to choose to yield to another. Submission remains the freewill right of the one choosing to yield. It cannot be demanded from another individual or imposed upon one person by another. When this occurs it stops being hupotasso and becomes domination." 10 Lies The Church Tells Women by J Lee Grady Published by Charisma House Charisma

Media/Charisma House Book Group, 600 Rinehart Road, Lake Mary, Florida 32746

Chapter 25

26   For further reading see Grace Revolution by Joseph Prince

27   Luke names some of these women who were both married and single; Mary Magdalene, Susanna and Joanna the wife of Chuza (Herod's steward) (see Luke 8:2-3)

Chapter 31

28   The Jews thought that to be the Son of the living God was a claim to be God Luke 5:21, John 5:18; 10:30–33.

Chapter 32

29   Discover Your Determination © 2019 Colleen McLean Westbow Press a Division of Thomas Nelson and Zondervan 1663 Liberty Drive, Bloomberg, IN 47403 wwwwestbowpress.com

30   Judaizers are Christians who teach it is necessary to adopt Jewish customs and practices, especially those found in the Law of Moses, to be saved

Chapter 33

31   https://www.christianity.com/church/church-history/timeline/1-300/a-look-at-the-early-church-11629559.html

32   "https://www.christianity.com/church/church-history/timeline/1-300/a-look-at-the-early-church-11629559.html